Jossey-Bass Teacher

Jossey-Bass Teacher provides educators with practical knowledge and tools to create a positive and lifelong impact on student learning. We offer classroom-tested and research-based teaching resources for a variety of grade levels and subject areas. Whether you are an aspiring, new, or veteran teacher, we want to help you make every teaching day your best.

From ready-to-use classroom activities to the latest teaching framework, our value-packed books provide insightful, practical, and comprehensive materials on the topics that matter most to K–12 teachers. We hope to become your trusted source for the best ideas from the most experienced and respected experts in the field.

i-SAFE Internet Life Skills Activities

Reproducible Projects on Learning to Safely Handle Life Online, Grades 9–12

JOSSEY-BASS
A Wiley Imprint
www.josseybass.com

Published by Jossey-Bass
A Wiley Imprint
989 Market Street, San Francisco, CA 94103-1741—www.josseybass.com

Readers should be aware that Internet Web sites offered as citations and/or sources for further information may have changed or disappeared between the time this was written and when it is read.

Jossey-Bass books and products are available through most bookstores. To contact Jossey-Bass directly call our Customer Care Department within the U.S. at 800-956-7739, outside the U.S. at 317-572-3986, or fax 317-572-4002.

Jossey-Bass also publishes its books in a variety of electronic formats. Some content that appears in print may not be available in electronic books.

ISBN: 978-0-470-53950-7

Printed in the United States of America.
FIRST EDITION

PB Printing 10 9 8 7 6 5 4 3 2 1

About the Book

In today's world, many life-skills tasks, from bill paying to applying for a job, are accomplished via the Internet. Before taking advantage of the many opportunities the Internet provides, it is important to know how to maintain personal safety and computer security while engaging in these tasks. *i-SAFE Internet Life Skills Activities: Reproducible Projects on Learning to Safely Handle Life Online, Grades 9–12* was written to address many of these tasks and activities that are frequently done online, and also to introduce you to some activities you may never have considered going online to do.

This interactive and empowering book of information and activities is designed for the high school student, college student, or young adult. The lessons can be integrated into schools, offered by clubs, or administered by parents. They are set up so they can be completed in a self-guided manner by anyone who wants to learn about safely handling life online.

The following chart provides the scope of the chapters in the book.

SCOPE OF THE BOOK

Chapter/Topic	Lesson Overviews
Taking Charge Online (Ch. 1) Computer Security Online Banking Online Research Skills Online Retail Shopping	**Computer Security:** Using the Internet for any activity opens you up to a variety of security risks, including risks to the computer and threats to personal security. This lesson covers four main areas of computer maintenance that can ensure computer security before engaging in Internet life skills: firewall protection, malicious code and anti-virus programs, system updates, and spyware removal. **Online Banking:** This lesson explores the benefits and drawbacks to online banking and gives you guidance for accessing actual online banking tutorials. You will learn about the risks of online banking and how to use technology to meet your own personal needs effectively and safely. **Online Research Skills:** The Internet is a vast resource that helps you find information about just about any question imaginable. However, it is important to realize that not all information found online is true, accurate, and valid. This lesson provides you practice in evaluating the authenticity of information found on Web sites. **Online Retail Shopping:** Shopping online calls for revealing private information that could be used inappropriately. Knowing the benefits and risks can make you a better, smarter consumer. This lesson explores the safety and security issues involved with online shopping and provides practice in selecting safer shopping options.

Your Online Persona: Using the Internet for any activity opens you up to a variety of security risks, including risks to the computer and threats to personal security. This lesson covers your online persona, including e-mail address, password, screen name/user ID, and personal Web sites.

Online Social Networking: Many people of all ages spend hours each day surfing and interacting on social networking Web sites. These sites integrate Web profiles, blogs, instant messaging, e-mail, music downloads, photo galleries, classified listings, events, groups, chat rooms, and user forums to create connected communities in which you are able to publish details about your life. This lesson covers the safety and security issues inherent to this new way to socialize.

Online Relationships: In this age of technology, you are bound to meet others while online and may develop ongoing relationships. In addition, many offline relationships use the Internet to communicate through e-mail, IM, chat, etc. This lesson covers the important issues involved in meeting someone new online or continuing an online relationship offline.

Online Gaming: Computer games used to be a solitary activity, for which your only interaction was with the computer or game console. Now, however, gaming has been revolutionized by the interactive community of online gaming. Features, such as voice chat, enhance and aid in the interactivity of this new medium. This lesson makes you aware of the risks associated with gaming activities and offers steps to take so you will avoid becoming an online victim.

Peer-to-Peer (P2P) Networking: P2P networking can be a beneficial way for you to interact with others and exchange pictures, word docs, and other media. However, P2P networking is best known for its illegal uses—illegal movie and music sharing, and more. This lesson covers the legal issues as well as the safety and security risks associated with P2P operation.

Putting the Internet to Work for You (Ch. 3) Online Search Skills Job Hunting Online Money Management with Technology Preparing and Filing Income Taxes Online	**Online Search Skills:** Is there any wonder Google is one of the most requested webpages online? You may already use search engines every day. This lesson helps you search more quickly and more accurately by teaching you basic online search skills. **Job Hunting Online:** More and more companies are recruiting candidates online using online job sites and online ad postings, or by searching online resumes. This lesson teaches you skills for effective online job hunting. **Money Management with Technology:** It is amazing how much you can do online with your money, such as pay bills, bank, and more. This lesson guides you through the money maze so you will have the skills to confidently manage your assets online and show you how to do so safely and securely. **Preparing and Filing Income Taxes Online:** Eventually everyone has to pay taxes. This lesson explains how to file online, the safety risks for you to consider, and whether you qualify for free software and filing.
Other Online Considerations (Ch. 4) Online Forms Online Communication Basics Working Wireless: Network Safety Considerations Public Wireless Access Considerations	**Online Forms:** The Internet is a wonderful place to shop, play games, conduct research, and more. However, many sites ask you to provide personal information in order to create an online identity, confirm identity and age, help to customize preferences, etc. This information is solicited via online forms. Online forms can make your online experience confusing. When is it OK to give out your personal information? When should you not do so? **Online Communication Basics:** There's more to communicating online than meets the eye. There are many risks, dangers, and pitfalls. We'll cover the numerous ways to communicate online and teach you what to watch out for. **Working Wireless: Network Safety Considerations:** More and more technology is going wireless. Chances are if you have multiple computers or a laptop at home, you've chosen to go with a wireless network. However, going wireless at home brings up possible security and safety concerns. **Public Wireless Access Considerations:** With a laptop computer and a wireless network adapter, you can connect anywhere there is an open wireless network. This includes public places that advertise wireless access, such as coffee shops, airports, hotels, and other spaces. However, just as there are security risks associated with home wireless networks, there are risks involved in using a public network.

Using the Internet to Move Forward (Ch. 5)	**What Do I Want to Be?:** High school is nearly over and you have to figure out where the rest of your life will take you. This step-by-step guide helps young adults figure out where they are going and how to get there. This section starts with determining what you want to do with the rest of your life and how you hope to support yourself.
What Do I Want to Be? Further Schooling Online Education: A Newer Option Applications, Scholarships, Loans, Grants, and More	**Further Schooling:** Teens and young adults either select a few careers they are interested in or know for sure what career goal they want to pursue. Does that career include further schooling? We discuss how you know what you need and where to go for more schooling. **Online Education: A Newer Option:** More and more accredited colleges are adding online or distance education programs. This section takes a look at the various levels of online education, potential benefits and drawbacks, and how you can learn more about different programs. Finally, we'll deal with how to select an online university. **Applications, Scholarships, Loans, Grants, and More:** Just as education has gone online and high tech, so too have the resources to apply to schools and financial aid. As you prepare to go to college—whether four-year, community, or online—chances are you will be online to apply, find financial aid, locate loans, and more.

This book has been extensively aligned to the ISTE's National Educational Technology Standards for Students referenced below:

1. Creativity and Innovation

Students demonstrate creative thinking, construct knowledge, and develop innovative products and processes using technology. Students:

- Apply existing knowledge to generate new ideas, products, or processes.
- Create original works as a means of personal or group expression.
- Use models and simulations to explore complex systems and issues.
- Identify trends and forecast possibilities.

2. Communication and Collaboration

Students use digital media and environments to communicate and work collaboratively, including at a distance, to support individual learning and contribute to the learning of others. Students:

- Interact, collaborate, and publish with peers, experts, or others employing a variety of digital environments and media.
- Communicate information and ideas effectively to multiple audiences using a variety of media and formats.
- Develop cultural understanding and global awareness by engaging with learners of other cultures.
- Contribute to project teams to produce original works or solve problems.

3. Research and Information Fluency

Students apply digital tools to gather, evaluate, and use information. Students:

- Plan strategies to guide inquiry.
- Locate, organize, analyze, evaluate, synthesize, and ethically use information from a variety of sources and media.
- Evaluate and select information sources and digital tools based on the appropriateness to specific tasks.
- Process data and report results.

4. Critical Thinking, Problem Solving, and Decision Making

Students use critical-thinking skills to plan and conduct research, manage projects, solve problems, and make informed decisions using appropriate digital tools and resources. Students:

- Identify and define authentic problems and significant questions for investigation.
- Plan and manage activities to develop a solution or complete a project.
- Collect and analyze data to identify solutions and/or make informed decisions.
- Use multiple processes and diverse perspectives to explore alternative solutions.

5. Critical Thinking, Problem Solving, and Decision Making

Students understand human, cultural, and societal issues related to technology and practice legal and ethical behavior. Students:

- Advocate and practice safe, legal, and responsible use of information and technology.
- Exhibit a positive attitude toward using technology that supports collaboration, learning, and productivity.
- Demonstrate personal responsibility for lifelong learning.
- Exhibit leadership for digital citizenship.

6. Technology Operations and Concepts

Students demonstrate a sound understanding of technology concepts, systems, and operations. Students:

- Understand and use technology systems.
- Select and use applications effectively and productively.
- Troubleshoot systems and applications.
- Transfer current knowledge to learning of new technologies.

About the Author

Founded in 1998 and active in all fifty states, i-SAFE Inc. (www.isafe.org) is the leader in e-Safety education. i-SAFE is a nonprofit corporation whose mission is to educate and empower students to safely and responsibly take control of their Internet experiences. i-SAFE provides knowledge that enables them to recognize and avoid dangerous, destructive, or unlawful online behavior, and to respond appropriately. This is accomplished through dynamic K through 12 curriculum and community-outreach programs. i-SAFE is the only comprehensive e-Safety program available that incorporates community outreach and youth empowerment in education-based materials.

i-SAFE's education component provides students with up-to-date, interactive, and age-appropriate e-Safety curriculum lessons covering a full spectrum of topics ranging from cyber bullying prevention and response to safety on social networking sites and the legal use of intellectual property found online. The prevention-oriented curriculum employs peer-to-peer communication and cooperative learning activities to help students retain this valuable information. The Outreach component facilitates the extension of students' newly acquired e-Safety knowledge beyond the classrooms and effectively raises awareness about online safety throughout the community. Youth empowerment is the link. Students are encouraged to become student mentors who communicate i-SAFE's online safety message via peer-to-peer contact and exciting community-wide activities, events and rallies. Since 2002, more than twenty-eight million students have been educated and empowered through i-SAFE's education and outreach programs to be safe and responsible online citizens.

At the same time, i-SAFE's professional development training prepares educators to teach the i-SAFE curriculum. Similar i-SAFE trainings for parents, for adults over the age of fifty, and for law enforcement educate and raise awareness about Internet safety in communities across the country.

Contents

Teacher's Guide

The complete i-SAFE Internet Life Skills unit is comprised of a series of five lessons addressing common life skills that are frequently completed on the Internet. This unit of instruction is designed to be integrated into career/life skills, technology curriculum, and/or general Internet safety and security instruction for high school and college-age learners. Each chapter includes student activity pages and a quiz. It is not necessary to complete the entire series in order to be effective—select topics that are most relevant to the student group. Workbook topics are set up to be completed by the student in a self-guided manner. The complete i-SAFE Internet Life Skills unit includes the following:

Chapter 1: Taking Charge Online
- Computer Security
- Online Banking
- Online Research Skills
- Online Retail Shopping

Chapter 2: Interacting Online
- Your Online Persona
- Online Social Networking
- Online Relationships
- Online Gaming
- Peer-to-Peer (P2P) Networking

Chapter 3: Putting the Internet to Work for You
- Online Search Skills
- Job Hunting Online
- Money Management with Technology
- Preparing and Filing Income Taxes Online

Chapter 4: Other Online Considerations
- Online Forms
- Online Communication Basics
- Working Wireless: Network Safety Considerations
- Public Wireless Access Considerations

Chapter 5: Using the Internet to Move Forward
- What Do I Want to Be?
- Further Schooling
- Online Education: A Newer Option
- Applications, Scholarships, Loans, Grants, and More

Understanding the Lesson Format

Each chapter is designed to help the student master a selection of basic online life skills. Each lesson is presented in sections to fully address the topic and meet the learning needs of a variety of learners. Lesson sections include:

- **Topic Overview:** A general description of the topic.
- **Vocabulary:** Critical terms and definitions used in the lesson.
- **Talk About It:** Provides thought-provoking questions. Depending on classroom setup, students can be directed to discuss with partners, in small groups, or as a class.
- **Free Write:** Supports exploration of the topic through a writing prompt and space to jot down thoughts and previous knowledge.
- **Think About It:** Reference information and materials to consider specific to the topic.
- **Activity:** Directions to complete either a directed or worksheet activity to support learning.
- **Go Online:** Provides an activity set up by the instructor to go online and apply what has been learned, by either researching a topic or completing a task.
- **Reaching Others:** Provides guidance for extending what has been learned by sharing this information with others.

Take the following steps to prepare for each lesson.

1. Review the lesson topics.
2. Familiarize yourself with the "Think About It" section, which provides students with direct reference information and additional sources to consider.
3. Prepare information for students on how they will implement the "Go Online" section. Section summaries are located at the end of the book to facilitate your preparation.
4. Optional: Prepare any additional reference material of your choice.

To implement each lesson:

1. Provide each student or small student group with a copy of the student pages for the lesson.
2. Review the lesson format outlined above (and also provided in the student pages).
3. Review any additional resource materials of your choice with the students.
4. Direct students to work through the lesson topics at the desired pace.
5. If desired, cover the Topic Overview, Vocabulary, and Talk About It sections as a large group before beginning independent work.
6. An optional quiz is provided to be administered upon completion of each lesson.

Additional resources

Additional resources are provided in the "Think About It" section of each lesson. Refer to the i-SAFE *i-EDUCATOR Times* newsletters, located under "Quick Links" at http://www.isafe.org and general i-SAFE lesson plans on similar topics for additional resource materials and background information, if desired.

Chapter 1: Taking Charge Online

Chapter 1, Taking Charge Online, includes the following lessons:
- Computer Security
- Online Banking
- Online Research Skills
- Online Retail Shopping

Understanding the Lesson Format

This chapter is designed to help you master a selection of basic online life skills. Each lesson is presented in sections to fully address the topic. Lesson sections include:

- **Topic Overview:** General description of the topic.

- **Vocabulary:** Critical terms and definitions used in the lesson.

- **Talk About It:** Provides thought-provoking questions. Depending on classroom setup, students can be directed to discuss with a partner, in a small group, or as a class.

- **Free Write:** Supports exploration of the topic through a writing prompt and space to jot down thoughts and previous knowledge.

- **Think About It:** Reference information and materials to consider specific to the topic.

- **Activity:** Each activity section includes directions to complete either a directed or worksheet activity to support learning.

- **Go Online:** This section provides an activity set up by the instructor to go online and apply what has been learned, either by researching a topic or completing a task.

- **Reaching Others:** This section provides guidance for extending what has been learned by sharing this information with others.

- **Self-Check:** A quick review to be sure you understand the concepts just presented.

 Additional Resources

Your instructor may provide you with additional online and/or offline resources to complete these lessons.

Quiz

Your instructor may administer a chapter quiz upon completion of the lessons.

Lesson 1: Computer Security

Section 1

Topic Overview

Using the Internet for any activity opens the user to a variety of security risks, including risks to the computer and threats to personal security. In addition, contrary to what many people think, computers are not designed to be maintenance-free. Just like cars, they need routine maintenance. And, like cars, they run better if treated well. To help you keep your machine running well and, better yet, running securely, this lesson will provide information about basic security maintenance skills and proactive prevention techniques for those who use the Internet.

This lesson covers four main areas of computer security maintenance:

1. Firewall protection
2. System updates
3. Malicious code and anti-virus programs
4. Spyware removal

Goal: The goal is for you (a) to understand the importance of the security measures discussed here and (b) to know the order in which to implement computer security protection measures in order to ensure that you are working in a secure computer environment.

Vocabulary

Familiarize yourself with the following terms and refer to this section throughout this lesson as you work through the activities.

- **Adware:** Another name for spyware.
- **Anti-virus software:** Computer programs designed to scan files and take proactive measures in order to prevent malicious code from attacking a computer.
- **Firewall:** A firewall is simply a program or hardware device designed to prevent unauthorized access to or from a private network by filtering the information coming through your Internet connection into your computer. Firewalls can be hardware, software, or a combination of both.
- **Macro:** A single computer instruction that results in a series of instructions in machine language. For example, you can program the computer so your direction "control-t" causes the font to bold, italicize, and center—one direction taking care of three actions.
- **Malicious code:** Malicious code includes any and all programs (including macros and scripts) that are deliberately coded to cause an unexpected (and usually unwanted) event on a user's PC. Viruses, worms, and Trojan horses fall under this category. Any of these types of malicious code can cause your computer to act up:
- **Trojan horse:** A Trojan horse cannot run on its own. It depends on tricking the user into running the program. It pretends to be something it is not. One common example: A user downloads and loads a freeware game. In addition to the game, the program also installs spyware or something else in the background which, in turn, runs on his or her computer.

- **Virus:** A virus is a malicious code that executes itself and replicates itself. For example, if you open an infected Word file, the virus will run and then try to infect other Word files on your computer (replication).
- **Worm:** To classify as a worm, the malicious code not only executes itself, but then attempts to make copies of itself from one place to another. For example, if your infected Word program then attempts to access your e-mail account and send itself in an e-mail to everyone on your address list, it is a worm.
- **Script:** In computer programming, a script is a program or sequence of instructions that is interpreted or carried out by another program.
- **Spyware:** Spyware is software that monitors and gathers user information without a user's knowledge and then transmits it over the Internet to a parent company. Spyware can gather basic information such as what webpages you view, your shopping habits, and so forth. It can also be used to gather e-mail addresses, passwords, and even credit card numbers. In addition, it can slow down your computer and your Internet connection as it transmits information.
- **Windows OS updates (system updates):** Windows operating system updates, also known as "patches," are comprised of computer code designed to correct weaknesses in your computer system.

Talk About It

- Have you ever inadvertently downloaded a computer virus?
- What were the specific effects?
- If you have not had experience with malicious code, what do you attribute that to?

Section 2

Free Write

It is important to make informed decisions about what you download from the Internet. Do you really trust what you are downloading? For example:

- You may not always receive what you think you are downloading.
- Downloaded materials may contain spyware.
- Downloaded materials may contain computer viruses that can damage your system.

Describe an experience you have had with malicious code or first-hand knowledge of another's experience with it. Do you know how the computer was infected? How was the problem solved? Based on that experience, would you recommend the same solution to someone else who wants to solve a similar problem?

Sample Free Write

I check e-mail regularly. However, Friday morning my e-mail box was full of messages. That morning I quickly scanned my e-mails. Hmm, besides the one from a friend I was expecting, another one catches my eye.

YOU ARE A WINNER!!! Wow—I wonder what I won, I think.

I open the e-mail.

It appears to be from a computer game software site. It notifies me I've won a free copy of their newest game—Tektronic.

All I need to do is download the attached game from the e-mail and install.

I am super excited. I don't remember signing up for any contests, but, hey, a free game is super cool.

I click on the attachment and download it.

It takes a few minutes to download, but then a menu pops up and asks if I want to install the program. Of course I click yes!

And that is when things go wrong—really, really wrong.

My computer starts doing whacky things. E-mail pops up and sends for no reason at all. A silly monkey pops up on his screen and does back flips while saying I GOT YOU!

And then, worst of all, the screen goes completely. . . BLANK!!!!

Oh no! What have I done???

I try hitting keys and restarting the computer. No luck—the same stupid monkey and blank screen.

I forgot one of the critical rules in e-mail—ensuring the source of the content is valid and reliable before opening or downloading an attachment!

Section 3

Think About It

As new operating systems become available, much of the responsibility for maintaining computer security will be covered automatically. However, at this time, most users are still on operating systems that require them to think about how computer security is being maintained and to take proactive measures to ensure ongoing security.

The challenge of maintaining a secure computer can be made easier by remembering the order of importance (steps) of security prevention measures. For example, a firewall is your best security defense; therefore, it is the first step. Each step after the firewall installation provides additional security, resulting in a well-maintained environment.

Step 1—Use a firewall: A firewall prevents information from entering your computer without your permission.

Step 2—Update your operating system regularly: Download updates for your operating system regularly.

Step 3—Use anti-virus protection software: Install anti-virus software on your computer, keep it updated and, most importantly, use it.

Step 4—Use spyware protection software: Install spyware protection software on your computer and run it periodically.

Think About It—Firewall Basics

All Internet communication is accomplished by the exchange of individual "packets" of data. Each packet is transmitted by its source machine toward its destination machine. Your computer, if connected to the Internet, is being attacked at least a few hundred times an hour by malicious data. If an incoming packet of information is flagged as potentially harmful by firewall filters, it is not allowed through.

Automatic protection. Many late-model Windows and Mac operating systems have built-in firewalls. For example, if you are using Windows XP, you have firewall protection. Additionally, your broadband service provider probably has firewall protection for its system. A firewall, depending on how it is set up, provides protection from a variety of computer security dangers, including some protection for malicious code and spyware; but, a firewall may not provide complete security protection. Windows Firewall, for example, offers protection from worms; however, it does not protect you from viruses or spyware.

Two basic types of firewalls are available: software or hardware. Software firewalls are ideal for single computers. Several companies offer firewall protection software. A hardware router—either wired or wireless—is the best choice to protect home networks that are connected to the Internet. The wireless router is ideal for notebook computers to provide mobility. However, only a few wireless routers come equipped with a built-in firewall, so you may need a wireless adapter. The wireless adapter acts as your firewall hardware. Once you choose and install a firewall, follow the instructions to make sure the settings are adjusted to meet your needs.

Activity

Analyze and/or research the firewall protection on a computer you regularly use (personal, school, or other) and summarize your findings. Include information about how you found your information. If you are concerned that your computer does not have a firewall, call your Internet service provider to check on the level of protection it has provided.

Firewall Summary
_____
_____
_____
_____
_____
_____

Think About It—Operating System Security Updates (Windows)

For purposes of this lesson, the security patch update example is for the Windows OS. Security patches are also routinely made available for Internet browsers and other software products. It's very important that you keep Windows up-to-date with the latest security patches released from Microsoft. These patches correct areas of weakness in your system.

Typically, an area of weakness is found, a patch is released, and a few weeks later a virus arrives on the scene to exploit the weakness. Those who have not downloaded the patch are vulnerable to breaches in security. For example, the catastrophic Blaster worm would not have been a problem if all users had been regularly updating their computers.

Use the Windows security patch information activity below to develop the general concept of how to update security with a patch. To be proactive in maintaining a secure computer, install updates as soon as new updates (patches) become available. You can configure your system to remind you to check for updates or, if you are connected through a cable modem, your computer can check for updates for you and notify you when they're available.

Activity

Learn how to update a Windows operating system.

- **To update a Windows 2000 computer OS:** Click the "Start" menu, select "Windows Update," and then, once the page loads, have it scan for updates. When that is finished, install all the "Critical Updates." The "Windows 2000" updates are optional.

- **To update your Windows XP computer OS:** Click the "Start" menu, go to "All Programs," and select "Windows Update." Once the page loads, have it scan for updates and then install all the "Critical Updates." The "Windows XP" updates are optional.

- **To update your Windows Vista computer OS:** Click the "Start" menu, go to "All Programs," and select "Windows Update." Once the page loads, have it scan for updates and then install all the "Critical Updates."

- **To update your Windows 7 computer OS:** Click the "Start" button to view the "Start" menu. Then choose the "Control Panel" option. Click the "System and Security" link from the "Control Panel" window. There is a direct link to the "Windows Update" option here in slightly smaller fonts, such as Turn automatic updating on or off, Check for updates, View install updates.

- **Option:** When you open the update window, there is an option to personalize Windows Update. Using this option you can set your computer to notify you of critical updates automatically.

Windows Update is a service provided by Microsoft that allows computer updates for Microsoft Windows operating systems and installed components, such as Internet Explorer, to be downloaded. Microsoft Update is an expanded version of the service that provides updates not just for the operating system and Internet Explorer, but for Microsoft Windows software such as Microsoft Office, Windows Live applications, and Microsoft Expression.

Windows Vista, Windows 2008, and Windows 7 all provide a Control Panel to configure update settings and check for updates.

Think About It—Malicious Code

Malicious code can be extremely harmful. These programs can change settings on your computer, delete files, slow down connection times, bog down e-mail, and more. One example is the ILOVEYOU worm/Trojan horse. It infected computers at more than half of the companies in the United States and even more in Europe. When it spread to a computer, it did two things: first, it overwrote files on the hard drive such as .jpegs. That meant picture files were overwritten with a copy of the worm and they could not be opened or recovered. Second, it installed a Trojan horse designed to collect passwords and transmit them to a server in the Philippines. The ILOVEYOU program replicated by sending itself to every address in every e-mail program it touched, causing it to also bog down the Internet.

If the computer you regularly use is not currently running virus protection software, it is imperative that you obtain and install this type of software. If running virus protection, make sure you update it frequently, as explained in the next step. An anti-virus program is an excellent form of protection, but is only as good as the most recent update. Even if you updated your definitions the week before a virus came out, you would be at risk until you installed the latest update that protected against that new virus.

Although this software is called anti-virus, most of these applications also protect against worms and Trojan horses. Most anti-virus software now have the ability to check incoming and outgoing e-mail (through popular e-mail programs like Outlook) to protect you against receiving or spreading unwanted computer problems through e-mail. Since Word and Excel documents are popular targets, most anti-virus software also specifically interfaces with these for protection.

Activity

Check Now: Take a moment to see whether you are running virus protection software. In Windows, go to "Start" (located in the lower left-hand corner of the task bar). Go to "Programs" and browse through your program list. Many programs are available. Common anti-virus programs include those provided by Symantec (Norton), McAfee, and Trend Micro (PC-cillin).

1. If you have one of these, open the program and familiarize yourself with it. When opened, many programs have an update button on the very first page.

2. The second step is to keep your anti-virus software definitions regularly updated. Most anti-virus software programs have a feature to automatically update your definitions periodically, and it's good practice to set this to update at least once a week.

Check Now: Go into your virus protection software and familiarize yourself with the options. See how to update the program and whether regular updates can be scheduled.

The installation of anti-virus software will protect your computer against malicious code that is sent via e-mail or is contained in Internet downloads. Even with protection, it is a good idea to be aware of suspicious e-mail. If you receive an e-mail with an attachment from a sender you don't recognize, don't open the attachment. Even if the sender is someone you recognize, don't open an e-mail with an attachment from him or her if you aren't expecting it or if the wording of the subject or message seems strange for that person to send you. It's a good idea to check to verify that it is legitimate. Also, make sure your anti-virus software is set to scan incoming e-mail automatically.

For protection from Trojan horses, be careful when you download and install any software from the Internet. If you do, be sure you are always downloading from a reputable site you can trust. Several sites offer reviews of the software you might want to download. Read the reviews to see whether other users have registered any complaints about Trojan horses or freeware in the software you are planning to install. Most major anti-virus software also now provide some protection against Trojan horses.

Again, set your anti-virus software to scan incoming downloads.

Think About It—Facts About Spyware

Spyware is a program that is typically loaded onto your computer without your knowledge when you download another program. The program gathers information about you and reports it back to a monitoring program, using your Internet bandwidth to do so.

Spyware can monitor a user's Web activity, scan files, create pop-up ads, log keystrokes, change the default page on the Web browser, and even gather personal information such as password and credit card information.

Caution!

Take care if downloading a program from the Internet; many advertised solutions are, in fact, spyware themselves. Find out whether that free program is recommended by credible, well-known sources. The safest way to find a good program, free or purchased, is to take the recommendations of reliable sources. Ask a friend, teacher, or co-worker whether he or she uses a good program.

Sometimes spyware is listed as "adware" in disclosure notices. So read carefully before downloading! In fact, many downloads advertise NO SPYWARE—but that doesn't mean you aren't bringing in adware!

Be proactive and guard against spyware! Obtain a spyware-removal program unless your anti-virus software also includes a spyware component.

Once you have obtained spyware-removal software, install and run the program according to the directions. Run a spyware check and removal once a month to eliminate these programs, as well as whenever you receive frequent ad pop-ups from a company or think something is slowing down your computer and Internet connection.

Activity

Run your copy of spyware removal software now. See how many programs are operating without your knowing it. Update the software to make sure you are fully protected. List examples of the types of spyware you found.

_____

_____

_____

_____

_____

Section 4

Go Online

Determine which section of this lesson covers your most serious computer security need(s). Select from the following options for an online activity.

Option 1

Visit http://www.microsoft.com/security/default.mspx and research computer security information. This site provides operating system updates, scans for malicious software, and no-cost anti-spyware removal tools.

Document what you did or what you learned:

_____

_____

_____

_____

_____

Option 2

Conduct an online search for more information and/or resources about anti-virus software.

List options and features that are available at no cost:

_____

_____

_____

_____

_____

Option 3

Find a comparison chart for various anti-virus programs. How do the free versions compare to more comprehensive software? Which option suits your needs and why?

Activity

Self-Check

Complete the following "self-checks" relevant to the security issues presented in this lesson. These activities are designed to be completed either for your own personal computer or for a school computer you regularly use.

- ❏ I know the order of importance of computer security maintenance measures.
- ❏ I understand the importance of a firewall.
- ❏ I know the status of firewall protection on my computer.
- ❏ I understand the importance of loading Windows updates.
- ❏ I am able to load critical Windows updates on my computer.
- ❏ I understand the importance of running virus protection software.
- ❏ I have a virus protection program running on my computer.
- ❏ I have run an update of my virus protection program.
- ❏ I have scheduled my virus program to run regular updates on its own.
- ❏ I know the basic difference between the various types of malicious code.
- ❏ I understand the importance of running spyware removal software.
- ❏ I downloaded or already have spyware removal software.
- ❏ I have checked for spyware with spyware removal software.

Reaching Others

Home	Community
If you have not used your personal computer for the lesson activities, check it for vulnerabilities to security attacks. Apply what you have learned by sharing information on computer security maintenance with a friend or someone in your family who can benefit from it.	i-SAFE provides a variety of programs to reach others with Internet safety awareness and education. Are you in a position to provide community service by teaching youth, parents, or community members about Internet safety? Go to http://www.isafe.org to learn more about educator, youth, parent, and community programs.

Lesson 2: Online Banking

Section 1

Overview

Why should you bother to learn about banking skills? What benefits are there for you? If you are in high school, chances are you have a bank account in your name somewhere. Perhaps it has been drilled into you all your life to put money you receive for holidays and birthdays into it. Maybe you have a part-time job after school and are saving for college. No matter what the facts are, someday you'll be out on your own and responsible for money. When that time comes, it will help to know some basics so you can make better choices if you opt to bank online. Additionally, perhaps you can teach your parents a thing or two!

Goal: You will learn safety and security tips for participating in online banking.

Vocabulary

- **Bank:** A business establishment in which money is kept as personal savings, for commercial purposes, is invested, supplied as loans, or exchanged.

- **Browser:** A program that accesses and displays files and other data available on the Internet and other networks, such as Internet Explorer, Safari, Netscape, or Firefox.

- **Cookie:** A collection of information, usually including a user name and the current date and time, stored on the local computer of a person using the Internet, used chiefly by Web sites to identify users who have previously registered or visited the site.

- **Encrypt:** To alter (a file, for example) using a secret code so that it will be unintelligible to unauthorized parties.

- **FDIC:** The Federal Deposit Insurance Corporation is a federally sponsored corporation that insures accounts in national banks and other qualified institutions.

- **Firewall:** A system designed to prevent unauthorized access to or from a private network. Firewalls can be hardware, software, or even a combination of both.

- **Opt out:** To choose not to participate in something, for example, having your personal information distributed by your bank.

- **Password:** A sequence of characters that one must input to gain access to a file, application, or computer system.

- **Secure:** Free from danger, attack, or loss.

- **URL:** Uniform resource locator—an Internet address (for example, http://www.isafe.org).

- **Virtual:** Created, simulated, or carried on by means of a computer or computer network.

Talk About It

- Explore what you know about online banking.
- What are some benefits of online banking?
- What are some drawbacks to online banking?
- Why would you consider accessing your bank records online?

Section 2

Activity

Directions: Fill in the Pros and Cons chart below with reasons you see for accessing banking records online and conducting banking business online.

Pros	Cons

Think About It

In general, there are three options when it comes to banking:

- You can go to a traditional "brick-and-mortar" institution that has a building and personal service representatives but doesn't offer Internet banking services.
- You can bank at a "brick-and-click" financial institution that has a physical structure and also offers Internet banking services.
- You can choose a "virtual" bank or financial institution that has no public building and exists only online.

Common pros of conducting banking services online:

- You can access account information, review bills, pay bills, transfer funds, apply for credit, or trade securities at your computer.
- You can use the computer to find out whether a check has cleared or when a bill is due.
- Some online banks provide better rates.
- You can apply for mortgages, shop for the best loan rates, and compare insurance policies and prices.
- Twenty-four-hour service and availability. You can access your account any time and anywhere (even while on vacation).
- No lines or waiting.
- Ability to download information into a software accounting program such as Money or Quicken.
- Ability to pay bills online, saving money for stamps and valuable time.

Section 3

Getting Ready to Bank Online

What should you look for and be aware of if you decide to bank online?

Obviously, PRIVACY and SECURITY are the most important concerns. When you bank online, your private information could be shared with others!

Read through these online banking tips and rules to stay safe and secure.

1. Review information the bank provides about privacy and security. Read it carefully. Look for the following:

   - Online banks might release information about your banking habits to other companies who want to sell you products. Review the privacy policy of your bank and check for an "opt out" clause.
   - Learn what the bank's policy is on using cookies. If, after you decide on a bank, you still want more privacy, change your browser settings.
   - Look for specific security policies. How does the bank protect your information during transmission and on the site? If you are unable to find this information on the Web site, call the bank to ask about its security policies.
   - Make sure the bank is insured by the Federal Deposit Insurance Corporation (FDIC). FDIC coverage only applies to deposits, such as savings accounts, checking accounts and certificates of deposit (CDs).

2. Security signs:

   - Is the URL a secure one? Check to see that it begins with https:// The s stands for secure.
   - **TIP:** Make sure all financial activity online is done via a **SECURE** site.
   - Does the site **encrypt** information that is sent? One way sites show this is via a small icon of a padlock or key during information transmission. It is often located in the lower right-hand corner of the page.

3. Conducting banking online:

   - Do not bank online unless you have taken the security measures learned in Lesson 1 (firewall, updated operation system, anti-virus, and anti-spyware protection).
   - Don't bank via wireless networks that are unsecured (Bluetooth, WiFi, etc.).
   - Choose secure passwords that are six or more characters long and a mixture of letters and numbers. Change your password routinely.
   - Any information, such as passwords or PINs that come from your bank in e-mail, should be changed immediately in case they were intercepted. Reputable banks will mail (not e-mail) this information.
   - Always make sure you are on the correct site. Imposters often create complex hoax pages designed to fool users.
   - Avoid communicating with your bank via e-mail, as e-mail is unsecured and can be intercepted.
   - Routinely check your account online for errors or discrepancies (at least once a month).
   - Report errors or problems immediately! DO NOT WAIT!
   - Don't have other browsers open while banking online. Some Web browsers temporarily store secure information from a Web site on a user's computer. Having another browser open could leave an avenue available for someone to access that secure information.
   - Exit the banking site immediately when finished with your task.

4. Ongoing security maintenance:
- Back up your files and keep virus software up-to-date.
- Don't reply or click on links in e-mails that appear to be from the bank.
- Never give out information via e-mail or phone to someone who says he or she is with your bank. Find a way to verify whom you are talking to.
- Be aware of other ways someone can gain your information such as by printed documents, using your computer, losing a flash drive with information, etc.

Your Protection

If you do EVERYTHING you are supposed to do (have a firewall, virus protection, report errors, and so forth), you are protected by the following laws if something bad does happen.

The **Electronic Funds Transfer Act, or Regulation E**, says a consumer's liability for an unauthorized transaction is determined by how soon the financial institution is notified. A consumer could be liable for the entire amount unless the unauthorized transaction is reported within sixty days of receipt of the financial institution's statement detailing the unauthorized transaction. The sooner the unauthorized transaction is reported, the less your level of liability; therefore, it's important to report unauthorized transactions immediately to limit loss. It is also important to remember that it might take time while the unauthorized transaction is being investigated for money deducted from your account to be credited back to it.

The **Truth-in-Lending Act, or Regulation Z**, governs illegal credit card use. While bank transactions conducted over the Internet are governed by Regulation E, credit card purchases over the Internet are governed by Regulation Z. When making purchases via the Internet, it's smart to use a credit card. That's because if a credit card is stolen or used by an unauthorized party, liability should be no more than $50 if proper notice is given to the credit card vendor. The vendor can be telephoned, but it's best to follow up the call with a letter stating that the transaction was made by an unauthorized user and detailing the account number and the dollar amount of the unauthorized transaction. Consumers do not have to pay the disputed amount while it is being investigated.

Go Online

Option 1

Go online and conduct a search using the term "online banking demo." Select one of the sample demos that comes up as a search return and run through the demo to learn more about online banking.

Option 2

Go to an online banking demo that your instructor chooses and run through the demo to learn more about online banking.

Talk About It

- What have you learned about online banking?
- What are the benefits and drawbacks?
- If you choose to bank online, what are some safety and security rules you should consider?

Reaching Others

Does someone in your family use online banking? Apply what you have learned by sharing online banking security information with a friend or someone in your family who can benefit from it. Think about it. You wouldn't want anyone you know or care about to risk losing his or her money when banking online.

Activity

Directions: Just for fun we've included a crossword puzzle to review the terms and rules for online banking with you!

Online Banking Review

Across

3. A program that accesses and displays files and other data available on the Internet and other networks

5. Federal Deposit Insurance Corporation

7. A system designed to prevent unauthorized access to or from a private network. Firewalls can be either hardware, software, or even a combination of both

9. To choose not to participate in something such as allowing your bank to distributed personal information about you

10. Free from danger, attack, or loss

Down

1. A sequence of characters that one must input to gain access to a file, application, or computer system

2. Uniform resource locator or Internet address (such as http://www.isafe.org)

3. A business establishment in which money is kept for personal savings, commercial purposes, investments, loans, or exchanges

4. To alter (a file, for example) using a secret code so as to be unintelligible to unauthorized parties

6. Created, simulated, or carried on by means of a computer or computer network

8. A collection of information, usually including a user name and the current date and time, stored on the local computer of a person using the Internet and used chiefly by Web sites to identify users who have previously registered or visited the site

Lesson 3: Online Research Skills

Section 1

Overview

Once upon a time, research was conducted by visiting a library, using a large card catalogue to look up a subject, hunting through rows of books to find the appropriate one, checking it out or—if it was an encyclopedia—making numerous copies. Now, however, a lot of research occurs online nearly instantaneously. Many schools still require print resources in addition to online ones, but we also do research for many other reasons beyond schoolwork. Think about it. Say you want a special recipe. You can go online, input your title or ingredients, and have an answer just like that. Or say you are dying to buy that new book that just came out but aren't sure whether your local book store carries it. Go online and find out.

The Internet is a vast resource that helps us find information quickly to answer just about any question imaginable. However, it is important to realize that NOT ALL information found online is true, accurate, or valid.

Goal: You will discover how to use the Internet for research that is both valid and reliable.

Vocabulary

- **Fact:** A real occurrence or something demonstrated to exist or have existed.
- **Opinion:** A belief or conclusion held with confidence, but not substantiated by positive knowledge or proof.
- **Reliable:** Worthy of reliance or trust; dependable source of information.
- **Research:** Scholarly or scientific investigation or inquiry.
- **Right to freedom of speech:** Civil right guaranteed by the First Amendment to the U.S. Constitution.
- **Valid:** Well grounded in fact or based on support.

Talk About It

- How can the right to freedom of speech along with the nature of the Internet result in inaccurate, invalid, and even dangerous information being posted as fact?
- What are some examples of why someone would post online information not based on fact? *For example: hate sites, drug proponents, sites to voice opinions, etc.*
- Why do we need guidelines for selecting Web sites in the cyber community?
- What can happen if we select sites with invalid information?

Section 2

Think About It

Anyone can post information on the Internet, which has resulted in easy access to many Web sites that:

- Contain inappropriate information
- Contain unreliable information
- Express inappropriate or extreme viewpoints
- Expose people to potentially unsafe situations

For example, take a site written by a Nazi sympathizer. Such a site might depict the Holocaust as pure fiction and myth. Information taken from this site for use in school reports could result in a poor grade, as it is not validated or based on fact.

Another example is that many sites that are set up as proponents of something typically depict the positives and skip over any negatives. There are many sites online for the legalization of various drugs. These sites loudly proclaim any benefits of the drugs but often fail to mention deadly side-effects and dangers. Using information that is biased without consideration of that bias could be dangerous.

Think About It—The URL

One of the first things to consider when evaluating a Web site is the home page's URL. The URL can provide valuable information and help you understand who is writing the web-page and its purpose.

Check out the following search tip-offs:

Informational Web sites: Web sites you use to gain knowledge about something—the purpose is to present factual information. The URL address of these sites frequently ends in **.edu** (sponsored by educational institutions) or **.gov** (sponsored by government agencies).

Advocacy Web sites: Web sites sponsored by an organization attempting to influence public opinion (that is, one trying to sell ideas). The URL address of this type of site frequently ends in **.org** (organization).

Business/marketing Web sites: Web sites sponsored by a commercial business (usually trying to promote or sell products). The URL address of this type of site frequently ends in **.com** (commercial).

News Web sites: Web sites designed to provide extremely current information. The URL address of this type of site usually ends in **.com** (commercial).

Entertainment Web sites: Web sites that provide entertainment such as games, puzzles, or music. Check these out carefully! Although many are created solely for the visitor's entertainment, a Web site of this type may actually be created to try to sell you an idea (Advocacy) or a product (Business), or to try to trick you into engaging in illegal or dangerous activity.

Activity

Brainstorm a list of criteria that should be examined to determine whether a webpage is useful, safe, and appropriate for its intended use, and then compare your list to the list on the following page.

Think About It

The following are items to consider in evaluation of a Web site:

- Author's name and qualifications and/or publisher or sponsor
- Contact address, phone, e-mail address
- Date created and/or date updated
- Source of information
- True information that can be proven with a print source or other Web site
- Layout of page, ease of use, fast to load, links that work
- Relevance or understandable to age group
- Age-appropriate content, that is, you would not be embarrassed if others knew you visited the site
- Minimal (does not detract from site's purpose) or no advertising
- Does not require personal information to use
- Free of charge

Section 3

Activity—Create a Web Site Evaluation Tool

Directions: Fill in the blanks on the following Web site evaluation tool with items you consider important for Web site evaluation. You will use this tool in the Go Online section of the lesson.

Web Site Evaluation Tool for Resources

Web site topic or name:

URL: http://

Section 1: Ease of Use

1. **Yes**   **No**   Is use of the webpage free of charge?
2. **Yes**   **No**   _____ ?
3. **Yes**   **No**   _____ ?

Section 2: Source

4. **Yes**   **No**   Does the information appear to be true, that is, can it be backed up or proven with a print source or another unrelated Web site?
5. **Yes**   **No**   Is it clear who is sponsoring the Web site?
6. **Yes**   **No**   Does the page contain information about the author's or sponsor's qualifications?
7. **Yes**   **No**   _____ ?
8. **Yes**   **No**   _____ ?

Section 3: Appropriateness and Safety

9. **Yes**   **No**   Can you view the contents of the webpage without giving out personal information such as name, age, e-mail address?
10. **Yes**   **No**   Is it clear why the sponsor is providing the site?
11. **Yes**   **No**   _____ ?
12. **Yes**   **No**   _____ ?
13. **Yes**   **No**   _____ ?

Notes:

_____
_____
_____
_____
_____

Rate the Web site by tallying the "Yes" and "No'" answers in each section.

☐ **✚ Recommended = Rates a "Yes" to all questions**
Note: No evaluation tool can be 100 percent reliable in evaluating whether a Web site is useful, safe, and appropriate for its intended use. However, sites that rate all "Yes" answers using this tool are probably reliable and appropriate.

☐ **0 Be Cautious = Rates a "No" to questions in Sections 1 and 2**
Note: Questions that rate several "No" answers in Sections 1 and 2 indicate that the Web site is poorly developed and may be unreliable and inappropriate.

☐ **X Not recommended = Rates a "No" to questions in Section 3**

Note: questions that rate any "No" answers in Section 3 indicate that the Web site is poorly developed and may be unreliable and unsafe.

Additional comments or considerations:

_____

_____

_____

_____

_____

_____

Go Online

Take time now to evaluate a Web site. We suggest looking at your district or school site to gain some practice in evaluation. Further practice can be gained by evaluating Web sites your instructor directs you to.

Talk About It

- How can evaluation elements differ based on what you are evaluating and the purpose for evaluating?
- Will your evaluation of a site differ if you are evaluating it for personal use rather than school use?

Reaching Others

Home	Community
Think about ways you can share your knowledge about online research with others who can benefit from it. Perhaps you have younger siblings or you advise younger students. Another venue is through school or public libraries. You could create an awareness campaign about safe online research skills.	i-SAFE provides a variety of programs to reach others with Internet safety awareness and education. Are you in a position to provide community service by teaching youth, parents, or community members about Internet safety? Go to http://www.isafe.org to learn more about educator, youth, parent, and community programs.

Lesson 4: Online Retail Shopping

Section 1

Overview

It's amazing what you can find online. Want a Spiderman collectible lunch box? You can probably find it on an online auction! Or how about some hot new name-brand designer jeans at a discount? Look online! Online auction sites and retail shopping sites are extremely popular. They help you find hard-to-find items and can save you money in the process. While online, you can book a hotel, send flowers, and even order groceries!

However, there are risks associated with online shopping. When you shop online you are revealing private information that could be used inappropriately. So whether you choose to shop online or not, knowing the benefits and risks can make you a better, smarter consumer.

Goal: You will be able to use the Internet to shop in a safer and more secure manner, as well as evaluate shopping sites to ensure they can provide a positive user experience.

Talk About It

- How many have shopped online or found items they wanted to purchase when online?
- How did the transactions go? Were there any hitches or problems?
- What do you consider possible safety risks of online shopping to be?
- What do you consider possible security risks of online shopping to be?

Free Write

Write a list of what you think can go wrong when shopping online. Take into consideration safety risks, security risks, and basic shopping risks. Consider when online shopping risks outweigh benefits and other cases in which benefits might outweigh any concerns.

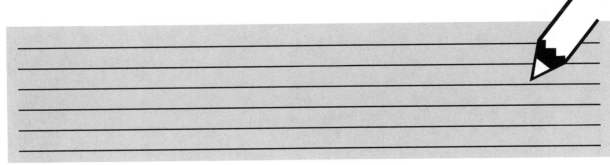

Think About It

Online shopping has some clear benefits and some clear drawbacks. Weigh them for each purchase you consider making and see whether online shopping works for you.

Benefits :)	Negatives :(
Twenty-four-hour access to shops	No storefront to return items or receive customer satisfaction.
Potential for saving money	Must reveal private information online
Larger selection	Not able to "see" item in real life
Ability to access reviews before purchasing	Fakes/frauds online—you can lose your money

How to Protect Yourself

- Shop with companies you know.
- Keep your password(s) private.
- Pay by credit card.
- Keep a record.
- Before purchasing, evaluate how the company secures your financial and personal information.
- Look for an online privacy policy and read it.
- Use the safety and security information from the previous lessons and apply it to online shopping situations.
- Online shopping sites are commercial ventures. Even reputable sites may use spyware (adware) to collect information about visiting users. Run your anti-spyware program after shopping on the Internet.

Activity

Directions: Sometimes it is difficult to judge whether a site you are interested in buying something from is valid. The best way is to prepare a simple checklist to evaluate a site. Remember the evaluation form you created in the previous lesson? We've modified it for shopping on the next page. We'll help you start. You fill in the remainder of the blanks with items you think are important for evaluating a shopping site. Columns on the right will be used in a subsequent activity.

Web Site Evaluation Tool for Online Shopping

Section 1: Ease of Use

1. **Yes**   **No** Is it easy to find information and what you are looking for?
2. **Yes**   **No** Can you find shipping costs?
3. **Yes**   **No** _____ ?

Section 2: Reliability

4. **Yes**   **No** Is the site known to be reliable? Why or why not?
5. **Yes**   **No** Is there a feedback rating system or another indicator of reliability?
6. **Yes**   **No** Does the feedback contain spaces for complaints as well as positive feedback?
7. **Yes**   **No** _____ ?
8. **Yes**   **No** _____ ?

Section 3: Money

9. **Yes**   **No** Can you pay with credit card or other secure transaction method?
10. **Yes**   **No** Is a return policy posted?
11. **Yes**   **No** _____ ?

Notes:

_____
_____
_____

Rate the Web site by tallying the "Yes" and "No'" answers in each section.

☐ **+ Recommended = Rates a "Yes" to all questions**
   Note: No evaluation tool can be 100 percent reliable in evaluating whether a Web site is useful, safe, and appropriate for its intended use. However, sites that rate all "Yes" answers using this tool are probably reliable and appropriate.

☐ **0 Be Cautious = Rates a "No" to questions in Sections 1 and 2**
   Note: Questions that rate several "No" answers in Sections 1 and 2 indicate that the Web site is poorly developed and may be unreliable and inappropriate.

☐ **X Not recommended = Rates a "No" to questions in Section 3**
   Note: Questions that rate any "No" answers in Section 3 indicate that the Web site is poorly developed and may be unreliable and unsafe.

Additional comments or considerations:

_____
_____
_____
_____
_____

Activity

Directions: Now you have a tool you can use to evaluate sites. Use it to evaluate the following three shopping options. Judge each site to see whether making a purchase would put you at risk for safety or security reasons. Are there red flags? Grade each "online purchase" as a good risk, acceptable risk, or unacceptable risk and explain why.

1. Review the following webpages.

2. Use the far right-hand column of the shopping site evaluation tool to evaluate each site.

3. Evaluate your comments and assign a grade.

4. Write a short paragraph to add additional comments or considerations explaining and supporting your grade.

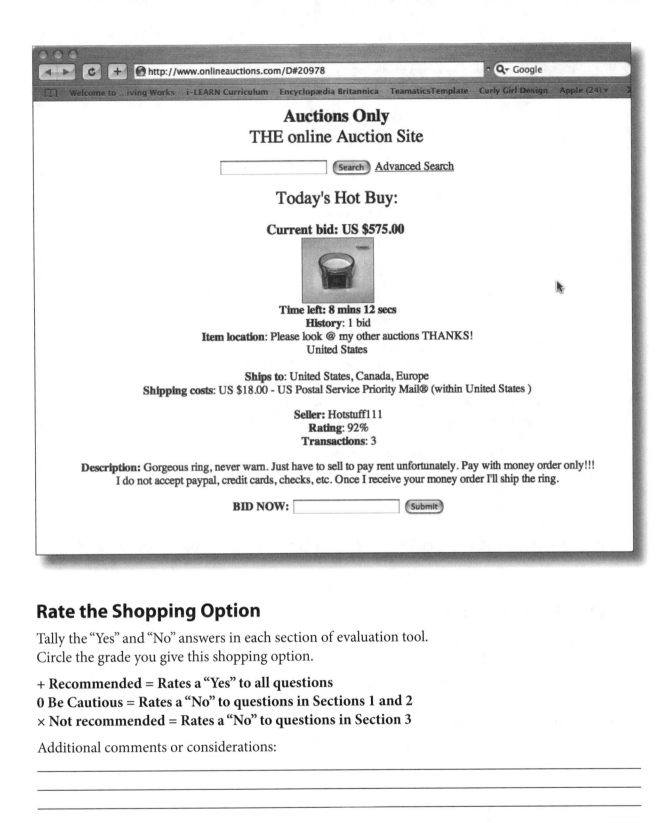

Auctions Only
THE online Auction Site

Search | Advanced Search

Today's Hot Buy:

Current bid: US $575.00

Time left: 8 mins 12 secs
History: 1 bid
Item location: Please look @ my other auctions THANKS!
United States

Ships to: United States, Canada, Europe
Shipping costs: US $18.00 - US Postal Service Priority Mail® (within United States)

Seller: Hotstuff111
Rating: 92%
Transactions: 3

Description: Gorgeous ring, never warn. Just have to sell to pay rent unfortunately. Pay with money order only!!!
I do not accept paypal, credit cards, checks, etc. Once I receive your money order I'll ship the ring.

BID NOW: [   ] Submit

Rate the Shopping Option

Tally the "Yes" and "No" answers in each section of evaluation tool.
Circle the grade you give this shopping option.

+ Recommended = Rates a "Yes" to all questions
0 Be Cautious = Rates a "No" to questions in Sections 1 and 2
× Not recommended = Rates a "No" to questions in Section 3

Additional comments or considerations:

_____
_____
_____
_____
_____

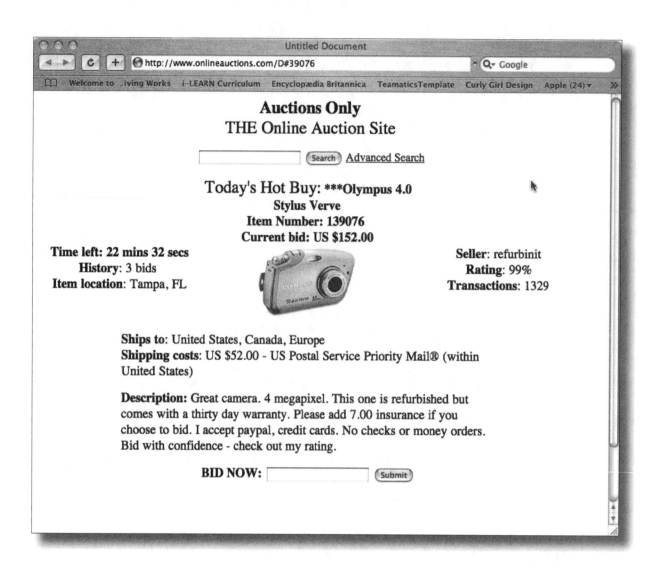

Rate the Shopping Option

Tally the "Yes" and "No" answers in each section of evaluation tool.
Circle the grade you give this shopping option.

+ Recommended = Rates a "Yes" to all questions
0 Be Cautious = Rates a "No" to questions in Sections 1 and 2
× Not recommended = Rates a "No" to questions in Section 3

Additional comments or considerations:

_____

_____

_____

_____

_____

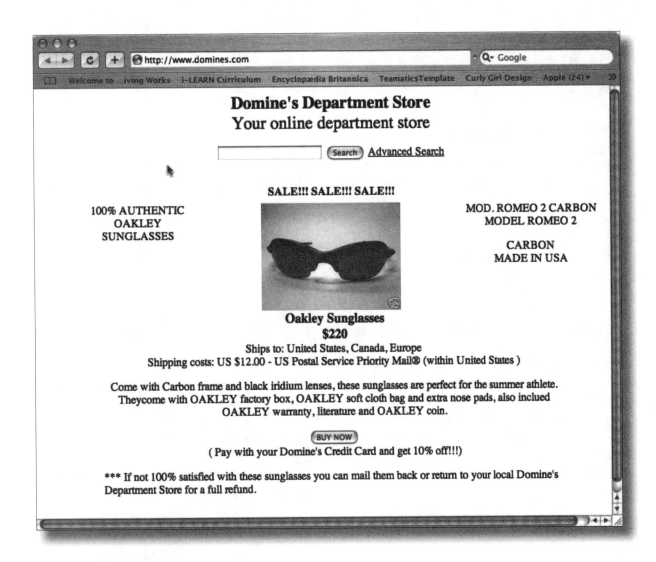

Rate the Shopping Option

Tally the "Yes" and "No" answers in each section of evaluation tool.
Circle the grade you give this shopping option.

+ Recommended = Rates a "Yes" to all questions
0 Be Cautious = Rates a "No" to questions in Sections 1 and 2
× Not recommended = Rates a "No" to questions in Section 3

Additional comments or considerations:

_____

_____

_____

_____

_____

Go Online (Optional)

Review an online shopping site selected by your instructor and rate it with your evaluation tool.

Talk About It

- Share your site evaluations and comments in class with your peers.
- Discuss what you have learned about online shopping and how to make smart and safe choices.

Reaching Others

Home	Community
Do you know anyone who shops online? Is he or she aware of the security implications? Apply what you have learned by sharing information about online shopping with a friend or someone in your family who can benefit from it. Provide a presentation on online shopping risks.	The i-SAFE i-PARENT program provides presentations and information for parents on online shopping risks. For more information, see http://www.isafe.org/channels/sub.php?ch=op&sub_id=2. To receive parent program materials, select the online Implementation Plan found on that page, fill out the required fields, and submit it.

Chapter 2: Interacting Online

Chapter 2, Interacting Online, includes the following lessons:

- Your Online Persona
- Online Social Networking
- Online Relationships
- Online Gaming
- Peer-to-Peer (P2P) Networking

Understanding the Lesson Format

This chapter is designed to help you master a selection of basic online life skills. Each lesson is presented in sections to fully address the topic. Lesson sections include:

- **Topic Overview:** General description of the topic.

- **Vocabulary:** Critical terms and definitions used in the lesson.

- **Talk About It:** Provides thought-provoking questions. Depending on classroom setup, students can be directed to discuss with a partner, in a small group, or as a class.

- **Free Write:** Supports exploration of the topic through a writing prompt and space to jot down thoughts and previous knowledge.

- **Think About It:** Reference information and materials to consider specific to the topic.

- **Activity:** Each activity section includes directions to complete either a directed or worksheet activity to support learning.

- **Go Online:** This section provides an activity set up by the instructor to go online and apply what has been learned, either by researching a topic or completing a task.

- **Reaching Others:** This section provides guidance for extending what has been learned by sharing this information with others.

- **Self-Check:** A quick review to be sure you understand the concepts just presented.

Additional Resources

Your instructor may provide you with additional online and/or offline resources to complete these lessons.

Quiz

Your instructor may administer a chapter quiz upon completion of the lessons.

Lesson 1: Your Online Persona

Section 1

Topic Overview

Using the Internet for any activity opens the user to a variety of security risks. Each time you go online, there is an inherent risk of contracting a virus, Trojan horse, or other form of malware. But there are other dangers associated with going online besides security risks to your computer. You also assume personal risk while forming and building your personal identity online. Are you opening yourself to unwanted attention, negative attention, or other risks as you interact online?

This lesson covers four main areas of online personal safety and security maintenance:

1. E-mail addresses
2. Screen name/user IDs
3. Passwords
4. Personal Web sites

Goal: The goal of this lesson is for you (a) to understand the importance of online safety and security measures that allow you to maintain your personal safety and security while maintaining an online persona and (b) to know how to implement those safety and security measures.

Vocabulary

- **Hosting:** Hosting is the business of housing, serving, and maintaining files for one or more Web sites.
- **Password:** A series of characters that allow someone to access a file, computer, or program.
- **Personal information:** Information that has the potential to identify you and/or your location.
- **Screen name:** The name you use to represent yourself online.
- **User ID:** Another name for screen name.

Section 2

Free Write

When you create a **screen name** and **password,** what do you consider? Do you frequently reuse the same password? Do you ever change your password? Why or why not?

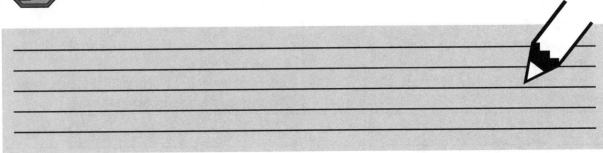

Think About It

The Internet is not anonymous, a fact that many of us often forget. When you sign on, others have access to you. Your e-mail address, screen name, and password serve as barriers between you and others online. You need to maintain this barrier by carefully selecting each of these. There are many out there who would like to know more about you for various reasons:

- Cyber harassment/stalking
- Identity theft
- Cyber predation
- Use of information to conduct their own business, either by selling your information or by using it in an illegal manner.
- Additionally, identifying information that you post online can potentially identify the location of your family members and place them at risk.

Personal (Identifying) Information

To maintain safety, the information listed below and other personal information should not be given out on the Internet.

name	home address
birth date	work location
age	city/location
Social Security number	school name

combinations of personal information such as listed above

E-mail Address

Unfortunately, although many of us "know" not to reveal personal information, chances are our e-mail addresses reveal quite a bit about us. Often our e-mail addresses are our names or other information that is quite identifying. It's time to rethink this choice.

User ID/Screen Name

Think about your own screen name. What does it say about you? When you choose a screen name, you want something that allows you to remain anonymous or unknown. Don't include personal information, and avoid suggestive screen names.

Change yours if it's unsafe. Use the information below when selecting a new screen name.

DO NOT USE	DO USE
<ul><li>your real first name</li><li>your real last name</li><li>your location (hilliegirl, HaverhillGuy)</li><li>your zip code</li><li>family or friend names</li><li>a suggestive name or word (sexyman69, hotbabygirl)</li><li>pornographic or obscene words</li></ul>	<ul><li>a nickname (sunshine, shortstuff)</li><li>something that relates to a favorite hobby, musical group, or movie (Cheering4u, LinkinParkFan, Matrixmad)</li><li>the current year added to the end of the name if someone is already using the name you want (shortstuff-99)</li><li>a second letter at the beginning or end of your nickname (ddancer instead of dancer)</li></ul>
For added security, always opt NOT to add your name or nickname to any sort of member directory.	

Think About It

Why Is password security important?

Many people like to "crack" codes and use e-mail for their own purposes. Some of these people may even be your friends or people you work with. People who crack codes use computer programs to do so. It is known that many people choose their passwords based on something personal such as name, address, Social Security number, phone number, and so forth. The program tries these first. Next, the program tries all the words in the dictionary forward and back. This only takes a few minutes. This is why it is unwise to choose a common word like "friend" as a password. Combinations of letters and numbers are a better choice.

Creating a Safer Password

Passwords should be a complex mix of letters, numbers, and symbols to avoid easy decoding. Try choosing a password that is six to ten characters long, unique, and a mix of characters and numbers. Then come up with a phrase or something to help you remember it. Don't write it down.

Additionally, it's a good idea to use different passwords for different Web sites. That's because if one of them is found out, access to your other information will not be compromised.

Password Tricks

So what are you supposed to do if you can't write it down and it can't be a word or familiar thing? There are tricks to creating a good password that can't be guessed, yet can be remembered.

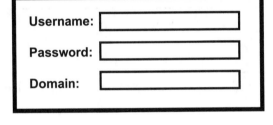

Here's one of the tricks: Take a phrase you like and will remember. Now use the first letter of each word. Add any appropriate capitalizations, punctuation, and other character manipulations. For example: "Three blind mice, see how they run" would end up as "3bm,shtr."

Activity

Brainstorm some password sayings following the example above.

1. _____

2. _____

3. _____

Section 3

Think About It

Personal Web sites have become very popular and are a great way of sharing with family and friends. However, many people forget that other people can see those same Web sites.

One of the best options for protecting yourself, your site, and your personal information is to password-protect your Web site. Give the password only to those you want viewing your site. This can eliminate many of the hazards of owning a personal Web site.

Even if you don't choose to password-protect your site, take some precautions to protect yourself and your identity. Also remember that anyone who conducts a Web search on you can find your site. This includes future employers, potential dates, and more.

See the tips below for personal Web site safety:

AVOID the Following	DO Take These Precautions
The use of your real name in your e-mail address	If you post an e-mail address, make sure it is anonymous (it does not contain identifying information).
The use of your real name on your site	Make up a nickname and stick to it when posting.
Posting personal information on your webpage such as phone number, address, birth date, etc.	Keep postings fairly anonymous.
Posting pictures	If you must have pictures on your site, password-protect the entire site so that only those you allow can gain access.
Blogging about your personal life	If you must blog on your site, password-protect the entire site so that only those you allow can gain access.
The use of a webcam or streaming video	Limit webcam use to family calls or interactions with personal friends, not for the public to view.
Posting your IM screen name or giving it out to strangers	Give your IM screen name only to those you know from the physical world.

Web Site Password Protection

Perhaps the easiest way to add password protection to your Web site is by using a free online service. All you have to do is sign up and add some code to your home page. Most of them work by simply giving you a code to add to your HTML after you sign up with them. This code creates a box for your readers to enter their user names and passwords so they can get to your password-protected pages.

Someone who comes to the page won't see the direct URL at the top in the address line. He or she will only see the link box URL, which provides a level of security. A user cannot go to the page directly and will always have to go through your home page. If you don't want a certain person to be able to access the page any more, you can block any user by changing the password and giving the new password to everyone else. However, if someone does obtain the direct URL of the page he or she will still be able to access it.

(Optional) Go Online

For more information and options for sites that will provide free password protection code, use your favorite search engine to search a phrase such as "download free Web site password protection" or go to the list of pre-approved sites provided by your teacher.

Your Digital Footprint

We're living in a digital age. Digital technology is everywhere. Some call it the "digital universe." If you think about it, probably nearly everyone you know goes online to shop, do school work, play, communicate, and so forth. On a broader scale, businesses now depend on digital technology to do everything from store immense amounts of data to facilitate monetary transactions.

When online, most people engage in activities that leave a "digital footprint." There are two ways of thinking about a digital footprint: (1) the amount or size—the actual bytes of information you create and place in the digital environment and (2) the type—the traces of activity you leave when in a digital environment. These join to make up your "footprints" that are left in many ways, such as joining a Web site, posting to a blog, releasing personal information online, sometimes simply by connecting to the Internet. You may not realize what information is being collected while you are browsing and interacting online.

From Walking to Running. . .

List things you do online that might leave a digital footprint:

_____

_____

_____

_____

Leaving a Digital Footprint

There are two types of digital footprints: passive and active.

A *passive* footprint is information collected without you really knowing, acknowledging, or even giving permission. Activities you don't even do online can also contribute to your digital footprint, such as a published article you wrote that shows up on a Web site.

List any **passive digital footprints** you can think of below (the first example is given):

- Cookies that track browsing habits
- _____
- _____
- _____
- _____

An active digital footprint occurs when you deliberately release information or post online.

List any **active digital footprints** you can think of below (the first example is given):

- Making an online purchase
- _____
- _____
- _____
- _____

Free Write

Why might someone care about his or her digital footprint? How can information left online be used by others?

_____

_____

_____

_____

_____

_____

_____

Caring About the Tracks You Leave

So why care about your digital footprint? Digital footprints can have big impacts that many do not consider. Some often-hyped dangers include the attention of stalkers, predators, and identity thieves. Information you leave online can be used for wrong or illicit purposes. While these things really can happen, of bigger concern are the more everyday occurrences that affect many more people. Consider the following examples:

Employers: More and more employers are looking at the digital footprints of potential employees to help evaluate the type of employee he or she might be. A December 2007 survey conducted by Careerbuilder.com found that 45 percent of employers reported using online search engines or social-networking sites to research potential job candidates.

Colleges and Scholarship Committees: Just as employers are reviewing digital footprints, so are those who approve college admissions and award scholarships. They want to see what the "real" youth is like versus the polished image seen in an application or interview.

Law Enforcement: As more and more people interact and communicate online, they leave traces of activities. Police cases are being made using information found online. Sometimes youth brag about exploits, post pictures, or even blog about activities that cross the line into being illegal.

School Employees: Some schools have clauses in student athlete, club, and other organization handbooks requiring a high level of behavior and standards to be displayed. Schools are using information found online as evidence—pictures of a wild party, for example—to suspend or enforce other disciplinary measures.

Businesses: Online retailers track business transactions of users, such as their e-mail addresses and the types of merchandise they buy or online loan applications. Sometimes they even buy this information from other businesses in order to send out e-mail advertisements.

> Your digital footprint is PUBLIC information accessible by anyone who wants to know. That could be your parents, the parents of your girlfriend/boyfriend, your next-door neighbor, your pastor, or anyone else. Think carefully about what image you are portraying online.

Think About It

What does your digital footprint say about you?

(Optional) Go Online

Try a few searches to see what your digital footprint turns up!

- Google your first and last name in quotes.
- Select another search engine and search there.

What about the digital footprints of others? Think about what your parents', teacher's, or even a community hero's digital footprint might be.

Taking Control of Your Digital Footprint

According to the Pew Internet and American Life Project, Internet users are now more aware that they leave digital footprints. They found that 47 percent have searched for information about themselves online, compared with 22 percent five years ago. But that doesn't mean Americans are trying to minimize or track their footprints. Few regularly check their footprints, and 60 percent say they are not worried about the amount of information available about them online. The reality is that many American adults may not realize how their footprints can affect their lives. Since youth frequent the Internet even more than adults, the potential for negative effects from their footprints may be even greater.

What can be done? Turn off the computer? Never e-mail or blog? Of course not! Extremes don't work and Cyberspace is a big part of our world!

Best Advice

Be aware of the image you present to the world. Understand that every time you go online you are contributing to your digital footprint—something anyone can see. Would you want everyone to see that photo you just posted or read the blog about your latest party? Be aware that the "you" presented to the world online can stick around for a long time. Work to present the best "you" that you can. And remember that minimizing personal information online helps reduce risks.

Think About It

Is there information you've posted online that you wish you had not posted?

What type of image do you portray online?

Have you opened yourself up to potential risk?

Cause and Effect

Read the stories below and then fill in the potential outcomes.

1. Janice, who is fifteen, posts a picture of herself drinking alcohol and making an obscene gesture on her social-networking page.

    Possible effects/consequences:

    _____

    _____

    _____

    _____

2. Mark, age sixteen, posts his e-mail address in order to gain access to a dozen online gambling sites.

   Possible effects/consequences:

   _____

   _____

   _____

   _____

3. Morgan regularly bullies another girl via text messages, on blogs, and on her own personal Web site.

   Possible effects/consequences:

   _____

   _____

   _____

   _____

4. Matthew provides his art portfolio on his social-networking page. He regularly enters his digital art works in contests online and has won several awards. In addition to contest Web site recognition, five online articles have published the contest results that mention his awards.

   Possible effects/consequences:

   _____

   _____

   _____

   _____

✓ Self-Check

Complete the following "self-checks" relevant to the Web search concepts presented in this lesson.

❏ I know the importance of not revealing personal information online.
❏ I understand how to compose a screen name that is safe and secure.
❏ I understand how to compose a password that is safe and secure.
❏ I understand how to develop a personal Web site that is safe and secure.
❏ I understand the consequences of my online digital footprint.

Reaching Others

Home	Community
Consider revising your personal screen name, password, profiles, Web sites, etc. Use the tips you've learned to ensure that you never reveal personal information when online and thus keep yourself safe and secure. Do you have a younger brother or sister? Review his or her screen name and help him or her to create safer ones if needed.	i-SAFE provides a variety of programs to reach others with Internet safety awareness and education. Are you in a position to provide community service by teaching youth, parents, or community members about Internet safety? Go to www.isafe.org to learn more about educator, youth, parent, and community programs.

Lesson 2: Online Social Networking

Section 1

Topic Overview

"Melissa graduated last week; I saw her photo on Facebook." "Let's chat on IM and discuss our summer plans!" "Did you hear who is coming to town for a concert?" "I heard the latest news on Twitter!"

Does any of this sound familiar to you? If so, you've already tapped into the wonderful world of social networking to keep in touch with your friends and associates.

Social networking Web sites integrate Web profiles, blogs, instant messaging, e-mail, music downloads, photo galleries, classified listings, events, groups, chat rooms, and user forums to create connected communities wherein users publish details of their lives. Many people of all ages spend hours each day surfing and interacting on social networking Web sites. It is clear that online communities are changing the way people socialize. Think about your own life. How often do you update or get updated online?

Goal: You will learn the basic concepts behind the technology of peer-to-peer networking and the associated safety and security risks by participating in such forums.

Vocabulary

- **Blog:** Blog is short for weblog. A weblog is a journal (or newsletter) that is frequently updated and intended for the general public to read. Typically, a blog reflects the personality of the writer.

- **Social networking:** Social networking is the process of expanding the number of one's social and/or business contacts by making connections through individuals. Social networking has gone high-tech with the advent of social networking sites.

Talk About It

- What social networking sites have you participated in?
- Have you faced any issues/problems on such sites?
- What are some potential issues/problems of social networking sites?
- How can these problems be prevented?
- How can problems that do arise be dealt with?
- Name some of the social networking Web sites popular with your peers.
- What are the benefits of socializing through online social networks?
- How might information obtained about an individual from a social networking site be used in a negative way?
- How might information obtained about an individual from a social networking site be used by a potential employer?

Section 2

Think About It

In addition to the positive aspects, social networking poses risks and shares information in ways the user may not approve of.

- Cyber predators use social-networking sites to "groom" potential victims through the use of posted personal information and communication tools.
- Information posted is in a public "space" and can be searched and viewed by anyone who logs on—friends, strangers, teachers, parents, parents of friends, and others.
- Identity thieves prowl social networking sites looking for victims to swindle.
- Information about you can be used by others to create a fake page or to bully.
- Comments online are, in essence, permanently recorded. Despite the casual and familiar feel of some networking sites, personal information is made available for people you may not approve of—to see or copy—and it is sometimes impossible to have comments erased from public view online.
- You may later regret a comment or photo that cannot be deleted. Most online postings, including deleted blogs, are archived and can be accessed for years.

Anyone who decides to participate in online social networking must consider all of the potential uses of posted information and take steps to ensure safe interaction.

- Review the site's privacy policies and check the site's default settings. Are you being taken advantage of?
- Do you really want or need to fill out that survey asking personal questions?

Find Out About It

How will your personal information be used by the Web site's owners?

- Review the site's user guidelines.
- Is there a code of conduct? Are there penalties for violators?

Review the Privacy Features

Choose the type of online community you participate in carefully. Review the safety options offered, such as the following:

- **Password protection:** Does access to the site require a password? Pick a difficult password to decrypt. Are there security questions to identify you when you forget your password?
- **E-mail address hiding:** Are there options to hide your e-mail address or only display a portion of it? Can others contact you without directly revealing your e-mail address?

Again, what are the site's default settings? Many sites show a lot of personal profile information as the default. You can turn these settings off and limit strangers from viewing all of your information by limiting access to your space to people you actually know.

Some sites have special privacy features depending on user age. For example, MySpace offers some privacy features that vary depending on the stated age of the user. Users under age sixteen can make their profiles private; the full profile can only be seen by pre-approved "friends." Remember, having a private profile doesn't make you invisible—other users can still search and find you by name or e-mail address.

Another option is to specify that the profile be made available only to MySpace users under eighteen. But remember that anyone can say he or she is under eighteen.

Most users of online communities can take other measures to protect themselves, such as:

- **Anonymous post blocking:** A feature on blogging sites that allows you to block anonymous posts to the blog (that is, the poster cannot remain anonymous if posting unkind messages).
- **Filtering options:** Another feature on blogging sites that allows you to set who can see posted messages.
- **IP address logging:** A feature on blogging sites that allows you to track each computer that posts comments on your blog.
- **Private communities:** You can set up private communities, which allows you to moderate and approve who joins, writes, or receives messages.
- **Alternate e-mail addresses:** Choose a free e-mail or alternate e-mail address for community subscriptions to minimize spam and scams.

Go Online

Visit the social networking sites pre-selected by your instructor and browse. Some sample sites include:

- Myspace.com
- Facebook.com
- Myyearbook.com
- Xanga.com

What safety and security risks do you notice? Do you see inappropriate pictures? Screen names? Blogs?

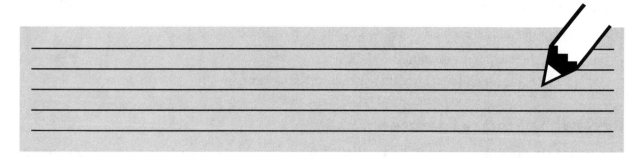

All Bad?

So are social networking sites ALL bad? Of course not! The benefits of social networking are well reported. They allow you to meet up and connect with others who share similar interests and ideas. They make it easy for you to reach across oceans and continents to find others who are like you. Social networks have changed history, such as reporting issues in third-world countries before traditional news outlets break the story. Networks have helped new businesses to be built and marketing to go viral. Studies are even showing positive health effects as people have built networks to support them in all kinds of crises.

Students like you are using online networks to launch their own product lines, to break into the world of writing and publishing, to gather support for important causes, and more.

Free Write

What are the benefits and drawbacks of participating in online social networking communities?

_____

_____

_____

_____

_____

Self-Check

Complete the following "self-checks" relevant to the social networking concepts presented in this lesson.

- ❑ I understand the benefits associated with participating in an online social network.
- ❑ I understand the risks associated with participating in an online social network.
- ❑ If I choose to participate in an online community, I know how to protect myself from safety and security risks.

Reaching Others

Home	Community
If you participate in a social network, review the information you have posted online and change it as necessary. Discuss this information with friends, parents, children, and others so they can make necessary changes if they participate in social networks.	i-SAFE provides a variety of programs to reach others with Internet safety awareness and education. Are you in a position to provide community service by teaching youth, parents, or community members about Internet safety? Go to www.isafe.org to learn more about educator, youth, parent, and community programs.

Lesson 3: Online Relationships

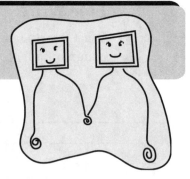

Section 1

Topic Overview

In this age of technology, online relationships are inevitable. Furthermore, many offline relationships utilize communication online through e-mail, IM, chat, and so on. There are important safety issues to consider, whether meeting someone new online or continuing an offline relationship online.

Goal: You will learn the positives and negatives in forming relationships in an online environment, along with how to pursue relationships in a safer and more secure manner.

Vocabulary

- **Forum:** An **Internet forum** or **message board** is an online discussion site. It originated as the modern equivalent of a traditional bulletin board and a technological evolution of the dial-up bulletin board system.
- **Instant messaging (IM):** A method of real-time communication between two or more online users based on typed text. The text is conveyed via devices connected over a network such as the Internet or cell phone.
- **Relationship:** A connection, association, or involvement.

Talk About It

- Have you ever participated in an online relationship of any kind (friendship, dating, business)?
- Why might some people find online relationships advantageous?
- How can/do online relationships develop differently than those created offline?
- What are some advantages of online relationships?
- What are some disadvantages of online relationships?

Section 2

Think About It

- Online relationships form through regular online communication, such as chatting, text messaging, bulletin posting, and so forth.
- Online relationships can have different goals, such as friendship, love, career networking, support community, etc.
- Online relationships come with both benefits and disadvantages. Brainstorm the benefits and disadvantages of online relationships.
- There are dangers involved in forming online relationships. Online communication has become increasingly popular in recent years, offering a way for you to meet and talk with others in an environment that seems anonymous and open. However, while it's

easy to meet people online, it is also easy to forget that these people may not be who they say they are or may not be there for the stated reasons/purposes they provide.

- What are some of the potential dangers?

- _____

- _____

- How can these dangers be prevented?

- _____

- _____

Talk About It

Consider the following questions and carefully evaluate your answers:
- What are potential benefits and risks of online relationships?
- When do the benefits of online relationships outweigh the risks?
- When do the risks outweigh the benefits?
- What are proactive ways to handle online relationships?

Remember the key concept that no matter what type of online relationship you are in, personal information should be safeguarded to prevent issues/dangers from arising.

Think About It

Chances are that if you're online, you've engaged in communication that helps develop an online relationship, whether that relationship is with someone you already know offline or someone you "meet" while online.

Safety Tips for Online Relationships

1. Treat all people you meet online as strangers, even if a friend has introduced you!
2. Take everything that's said online with a grain of salt. It is all too easy to develop a new persona or make things up when online.
3. There are many ways to deceive online. Be aware that the person on the other end may or may not be there for the same reasons you are.
4. Don't give out personal details, such as your name, phone number, address, or a personal description, to people with whom you chat on the Internet. Even if the person is who he or she says and not a predator, relationships that end badly can degenerate into cyber harassment or stalking.
5. Trust your instincts. If you feel uneasy about someone, there may be a reason. Get out of the relationship. Get help from someone you know offline, if needed.

Activity

A mnemonic is a device to help you remember critical information. One common mnemonic for remembering lists consists of an easily remembered acronym or phrase with an acronym that is associated with the list items. For example, to remember the colors of the rainbow (Red, Orange, Yellow, Green, Blue, Indigo, Violet), it can be easier for some people to remember the mnemonic "Roy G. Biv" (a made-up name) instead.

Now create your own mnemonic to remember the above safety tips on Internet relationships:

_____

_____

_____

_____

Types of Online Relationships

- **Friendship:** basic friendship, discuss daily events, hang out
- **Special Interests:** clubs and hobbies
- **Support Group:** friendship based on central issue (health problem, new baby)
- **Dating:** online dating that may progress to physical meeting
- **Business/Professional:** interaction for the purpose of getting ahead in business or school

Activity

For each of the types of online relationships listed above, answer the following questions:
- How do such relationships form online?
- What types of communication can occur in such an online relationship?
- What are some benefits of this type of online relationship?
- What are some drawbacks/dangers of this type of online relationship?
- Compose a safety tip/rule specific to this type of relationship.

Friendship:

_____

_____

_____

_____

_____

Special Interest:

_____

_____

_____

_____

_____

Support:

_____
_____
_____
_____
_____
_____

Dating:

_____
_____
_____
_____
_____
_____

Professional:

_____
_____
_____
_____
_____
_____

Which of these relationships would you consider participating in online? Why?

_____
_____
_____
_____
_____

Self-Check

Complete the following "self-checks" relevant to the online relationship concepts presented in this lesson.

❏ I understand the different types of online relationships.

❏ I understand how to participate in safe online relationships.

❏ I understand the benefits and drawbacks of online relationships.

Reaching Others

Home	Community
Think about ways you can share your knowledge about online relationships with others who can benefit from it. Perhaps you have younger siblings or you are in a position to advise younger students. Another venue is through school or public libraries. If so, create an awareness campaign about safe online relationships and their benefits and risks.	i-SAFE provides a variety of programs to reach others with Internet safety awareness and education. Are you in a position to provide community service by teaching youth, parents, or community members about Internet safety? Go to www.isafe.org to learn more about educator, youth, parent, and community programs.

Lesson 4: Online Gaming

Computer games used to be a solitary activity, where the only interaction was with the computer or game console. Now, however, gaming has been revolutionized by the interactive community-building features available online. New features, such as voice chat, enhance and aid in the interactivity of this new medium. As with any type of online interaction, when you participate in online gaming you need to be aware of the dangers and risks and take steps to prevent becoming an online victim.

Goal: You will discover basic safety and security tips for better online gaming experiences.

Vocabulary

- **Griefer:** A player who plays a computer game in order to irritate and harass other players, rather than in pursuit of game objectives
- **Netiquette:** Stands for "Internet etiquette" and refers to the set of practices developed over the years to make the Internet experience pleasant for everyone.
- **Newbie:** One who is new to an online venue such as a game or chat room.
- **Online gaming:** Internet games that are played online. Normally, all that is required to play Internet games are a Web browser and the appropriate plugin (normally available for free via the plugin maker's Web site). A game played in a browser is often called a browser-based game.

Talk About It

- Do you play computer games?
- Have you engaged in interactive online gaming?
- Have you ever used voice chat in gaming?
- What are some potential risks associated with gaming?
- What are some potential benefits associated with gaming?

Online video games aren't just for kids anymore. Online gaming is a multi-billion-dollar business. No longer are you limited to just playing with your friends in the same room or competing against a computer; now you can play with others from around the world. While most online gamers are between sixteen and twenty-five, it is more and more common to see online games for pre-teens. Most players are online to have fun and play games with people who have similar interests, but an online game could be an open invitation for a predator—an issue that most online gaming companies try to downplay. Online games do not pose as many dangers as blogs or chat rooms; they do, however, offer an avenue for young people to interact and talk with strangers. You really don't know who is on the other end of your conversation.

Think About It

Games run the gamut from shoot-em-ups to role playing and more. The online environment allows a chance for you to interact with others who have similar interests. Currently, most online gaming communities attract serious players. But as online gaming grows in popularity, newbies will gather and more issues will pop up.

Youth are attracted to many facets of the online gaming concept. It allows the option to play a role; the interaction can help build a sense of community and can give you a sense of power and identity. However, you can also become addicted to gaming or become involved in inappropriate games, such as those that are excessively violent.

- Why are violent games of concern?
- What are some benefits of online gaming?
- What are some drawbacks of online gaming?

Online Gaming Risks

Just like any online activity that involves interaction, online gaming comes with risks and security concerns. These include cyber bullying and harassment, cyber predators, and other crimes of victimization.

Online gaming comes with some prevention tips/rules of its own. While the standard rules still apply (don't reveal personal information, don't meet offline, and so forth) these don't cover every facet of this unique environment.

For example, if involved in games that have voice chat enabled, you are automatically revealing certain amounts of personal information, such as approximate age and gender.

Another issue is that the intimacy of voice chat leads many players to feel they really know the people they interact with. As a result, some barriers are broken down and it seems easier to give out information, such as a phone number. After all, they are already chatting via a microphone, so how is a phone much different?

How is talking via voice chat different from giving out a phone number?

_____
_____
_____
_____

With a phone number, what information can be discovered about you?

_____
_____
_____
_____

Safety Tips Geared Specifically Toward Online Gaming Communities

1. **Educate yourself:** Different games/communities have different privacy statements and terms of acceptable use. Know what you can do if you get into trouble. Can you contact a site administrator? Block participants?

2. **Ensure privacy:** Use privacy features that gaming sites offer. For example, if a game offers voice masking, use it to disguise your voice. In addition, don't reveal private information or post pictures.

3. **Choose appropriate names:** Choose a suitable screen or character name when playing. Don't reveal personal information or invite harassment.

4. **Play wisely:** If you feel uncomfortable during a game, log off. If language becomes inappropriate, block the offender's chat capabilities so you do not hear it and then report that person.

5. **Don't reveal screen names/passwords:** If you give screen names/passwords to offline or online friends, they could log in as you. You don't want anyone playing as you.

Griefers or Cheesers

A lot of playgrounds have bullies—even the virtual ones. If you play online games, you've probably met them. Also known as "griefers" or "cheesers," these bullies get their jollies from messing up online multiplayer game sites like Halo 2, EverQuest, or The Sims Online. Griefers scam, cheat, abuse, and often victimize the weakest and newest players in the online game community. Whether it's stealing health potions or blocking passage to important areas, griefers spoil the fun and frustrate everybody. How do you deal with them? Here are some useful tips that every gamer—no matter what age group— should know about handling cyber bullies.

1. **Pay them no mind.** Griefers want to get a rise out of you. That's why they do what they do. More often than not, the easiest way to get rid of them is by ignoring them. Many will eventually get bored and go away.

2. **Give it a rest.** By nature, griefers are a fickle bunch. Sometimes the best way to rid yourself of their unwanted attention is by simply quitting the game or switching to another one. If a cyber bully's favorite victim seems to have moved on, frequently they do, too.

3. **Go easy.** Never act out of anger or use griefers' own strategies against them. Why stoop to their level? This could prompt an even bigger blow-up and, worse yet, label you as a griefer.

4. **Don't get personal.** If they are given access to your name, phone number, or e-mail address, harassment may spill over into the real world. Guard yourself by using handles (online nicknames) and passwords unique to each game, and always keep personal information concealed.

5. **Consider your options.** Many games allow you to restrict communication only to those on your exclusive, preprogrammed friends list. Others offer opportunities for turning off features (friendly fire options, permanents knockouts) that can be exploited by griefers.

6. **No trash talking.** Many games encourage making fun of opponents. Take a pass on those games. If you are out there calling people names or making jokes at others' expense, chances are that, sooner or later, someone will be offended.

7. **Finally, remember you have full control over which games you play.** Select those that are well supervised and have strict rules or enforceable codes of conduct. Many game publishers are starting to employ full-time staffers to deal with griefers. If someone starts causing problems, there is someone to turn to.

Activity: Develop a Creed

A **creed** is a system of beliefs or principles.

Directions: Based on what you know about online gaming, develop a creed to help keep online gamers safe and fun. Be sure to cover basic rules: cyber harassment, netiquette, and more in your creed.

_____

_____

_____

_____

_____

_____

Go Online

Many online sites that can be used to evaluate games. These sites help you make critical decisions on whether the codes of conduct and rules for the games are appropriate, have risks involved in playing, and more.

The site http://www.commonsensemedia.org can be used by parents to determine whether sites are valid, reliable, and safe for their children. Many other sites are available to help you review gaming sites that are more appropriate for teenagers and young adults. Take a search online and find some great review sites.

1. _____
2. _____
3. _____

Self-Check

Complete the following "self-checks" relevant to the Web search concepts presented in this lesson.

❑ I understand how online gaming can work.

❑ I understand how to protect myself if I participate in online gaming.

❑ I understand the risks associated with online gaming.

Reaching Others

Home	Community
Do you know anyone who games online? Is he or she aware of the safety and security implications? Apply what you have learned by sharing information on online gaming with a friend or someone in your family who can benefit from it.	i-SAFE provides a variety of programs to reach others with Internet safety awareness and education. Are you in a position to provide community service by teaching youth, parents, or community members about Internet safety? Go to www.isafe.org to learn more about educator, youth, parent, and community programs.

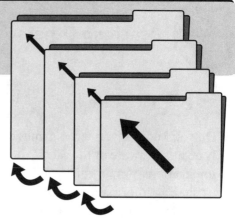

Lesson 5: Peer-to-Peer (P2P) Networking

Section 1

Topic Overview

Just what is peer-to-peer networking (P2P)? P2P is a concept similar to the use of an Internet browser, such as Firefox, Internet Explorer, or others. It is an application that runs on your computer and allows you to share files with others around the world. You share your files and you access the files of others.

P2P networking can be a beneficial way of interacting with others and exchanging files, such as pictures, Word documents, and more. However, P2P networking is best known for its illegal uses—such as movie and music sharing. There are also risks to personal safety and computer security associated with P2P operation.

Goal: You will learn the basic concepts behind P2P technology and the associated safety and security risks when participating in P2P networking.

Vocabulary

- **File sharing:** The practice of distributing or providing access to digitally stored information, such as computer programs, multi-media (audio/video), documents, or electronic books. It may be implemented in a variety of storage, transmission, and distribution models. Common methods are manual sharing using removable media, centralized computer file server installations on computer networks, Web-based documents, and the use of distributed peer-to-peer (P2P) networking.
- **P2P network:** Peer-to-peer (referred to as P2P) is a type of transient Internet network that allows a group of computer users with the same networking program or software to connect with each other and directly access files from one another's hard drives.

Talk About It

- Do you have file-sharing software on your computer?
- Have you ever used file-sharing software?
- What did you use the software for?
- Define in your own words what file sharing is.
- What are some security risks associated with file sharing?
- How can intellectual property rights such as copyright issues be impacted by file-sharing software?
- What are some legitimate uses of P2P software?

Section 2

Think About It

Peer-to-peer (P2P) file sharing allows you to share files online through an informal network of computers running the same software. File sharing can give you access to a wealth of information, but it also has a number of risks. You could download copyright-protected material, pornography, or viruses without meaning to. Or you could mistakenly allow other people to copy files you don't mean to share, such as confidential documents or even your entire hard-drive!

If you are considering P2P file sharing:

- Set up the file-sharing software very carefully, checking the proper settings so that other users won't have access to your private files.
- You may want to adjust the file-sharing program's controls so that it is not connected to the P2P network all the time. Some file-sharing programs automatically open every time you turn on your computer.
- Use anti-virus software and a firewall, and keep them up-to-date. Files you download using a P2P network could be mislabeled, hiding a virus or other unwanted content. (Information about firewalls and anti-virus software can be found in Chapter 1.)
- Install anti-spyware software. Some file-sharing programs install spyware that can monitor your browsing habits and send that data to third parties. (Information about spyware can be found in Chapter 1.)
- Think about service overload. When you download files, you are eating up bandwidth. Others may be downloading from you at the same time, which could result in a slowing of your computer.
- Understand intellectual property concerns. The material you can obtain from file sharing isn't necessarily "free and clear." It may be copyrighted or pirated, which means you're breaking the law when you download it without buying it. You could be faced with hefty fines or other legal action. For example, the music industry has pursued many lawsuits against people who have downloaded music files illegally.

Free Write

- There are over 150 million users of P2P software. (per Internetfilterreview.com)
- Students twelve to eighteen years make up 41 percent of American P2P users. (per Recording Industry Association of America)
- Fifty-six percent of files found while using innocent search terms were pornographic. (per U.S. House Committee on Government Reform and General Accounting Office)

Based on the above stats, jot down your thoughts concerning P2P networking.

Think About It

Over 150 million people worldwide use P2P software. However, not all of these people are safe, responsible, law-abiding citizens.

There are a number of reasons why P2P file sharing is so dangerous:

- **Illegal, unethical, and immoral:** Unfortunately, the most common uses of P2P are illegal ones, such as downloading copyrighted music, copyrighted software, pornographic material, and even child pornography.

- **Viruses:** When downloading a shared file, there is the danger of downloading a computer virus or Trojan horse onto your computer. These viruses can cause all kinds of problems, such as erasing all the files on the hard drive or automatically sending pornographic e-mails to all of your friends in your mail directory. The worst part is that virus protection software works on the Internet and e-mail, but doesn't protect you while you run P2P software.

- **Pornographic downloads:** Today, 35 percent of all P2P downloads are related to pornographic material. This equates to approximately 1.5 billion pornographic file downloads every month. When children access a pornographic Web site, what they usually view are a number of still photographs of objectionable material. The really bad, most graphic material is usually not available unless it is purchased with a credit card. With P2P file sharing, children can download a free XXX-rated movie full of hard-core pornography. What's more, most Internet filters don't work well or often not at all with P2P software.

- **Spyware:** Many of the P2P programs automatically install spyware on your computer as part of the installation process. These spyware programs can range from a simple nuisance to a true invasion of privacy. They can cause numerous pop-up ads or banners to appear, install tracking programs that view your usage patterns, and more. If you notice that you are receiving numerous annoying pop-up messages, you may have a P2P file-sharing program installed on your computer.

- **Piracy:** Perhaps the most common use of P2P networks is the sharing and exchanging of pirated material. This use has been brought into the spotlight with court cases in which the music industry has prosecuted and fined people who downloaded copyrighted material.

Go Online

In late June of 2005, the Supreme Court made a landmark ruling on the use of peer-to-peer networks. The case is known as MGM vs. Grokster. Go online and research the Court's ruling.

In your own words, write a short summary that describes the ruling.

_____

_____

_____

_____

_____

Think About It

Based on the MGM vs. Grokster ruling, the music and movie industry can now take software and technology designers to court for the court to decide whether the software program promotes or fosters illegal file sharing.

Possible Consequences to Consider

- It is expected that the format will need to be changed to monitor content in some way or legalize downloads. Others may charge fees or have other requirements.
- Users may see many peer-to-peer networks disappear rather than try to change to abide by new rules.
- It has been suggested that the cost of lawsuits and the threat of expensive court cases could force many tech companies to go out of business.

Think About It

- How do cyber ethics dictate one's actions in conjunction with file-sharing networks?
- Consider each of the following items under "The Conflict." How does each of these items cause a breakdown in cyber ethics? Then answer the questions under "Ethics and File Sharing."

The Conflict

- The Internet allows for immediate availability of some "really cool" stuff.
- It is fairly easy to obtain this cool stuff.
- There aren't any Internet police, per se (the Internet is a global community).
- In some areas of the world, laws about intellectual property use on the Internet are still being written.
- Victims of file sharing are distant and not face-to-face.

_____

_____

_____

_____

_____

_____

Ethics and File Sharing

- Why do people use file-sharing software?
- What are legitimate uses of the software?
- What are illegal uses of the software?
- What are risks associated with using this software?

_____

_____

_____

_____

_____

_____

Go Online

Research the legal consequences of file sharing with regard to intellectual property concerns and copyright violation.

Self-Check

Complete the following "self-checks" relevant to the concepts presented in this lesson.

❑ I understand the legal ramifications of using P2P networks.

❑ I understand the legal uses of P2P software.

❑ I understand how P2P software can be used illegally.

❑ I understand both the safety and security risks of using P2P software.

Reaching Others

Home	Community
Do you know anyone who chooses to use P2P software? Is he or she aware of the safety and security implications? Does he or she use the software for legal or illegal purposes? Apply what you have learned by sharing information on P2P networks with a friend or someone in your family who can benefit from it.	i-SAFE provides a variety of programs to reach others with Internet safety awareness and education. Are you in a position to provide community service by teaching youth, parents, or community members about Internet safety? Go to www.isafe.org to learn more about educator, youth, parent, and community programs.

Chapter 3: Putting the Internet to Work for You

Chapter 3, Putting the Internet to Work for You, includes the following lessons:

- Online Search Skills
- Job Hunting Online
- Money Management with Technology
- Preparing and Filing Income Taxes Online

Understanding the Lesson Format

This chapter is designed to help you master a selection of basic online life skills. Each lesson is presented in sections to fully address the topic. Lesson sections include:

- **Topic Overview:** General description of the topic.

- **Vocabulary:** Critical terms and definitions used in the lesson.

- **Talk About It:** Provides thought-provoking questions. Depending on classroom setup, students can be directed to discuss with a partner, in a small group, or as a class.

- **Free Write:** Supports exploration of the topic through a writing prompt and space to jot down thoughts and previous knowledge.

- **Think About It:** Reference information and materials to consider specific to the topic.

- **Activity:** Each activity section includes directions to complete either a directed or worksheet activity to support learning.

- **Go Online:** This section provides an activity set up by the instructor to go online and apply what has been learned, either by researching a topic or completing a task.

- **Reaching Others:** This section provides guidance for extending what has been learned by sharing this information with others.

- **Self-Check:** A quick review to be sure you understand the concepts just presented.

Additional Resources

Your instructor may provide you with additional online and/or offline resources to complete these lessons.

Quiz

Your instructor may administer a chapter quiz upon completion of the lessons.

Lesson 1: Online Search Skills

Section 1

Topic Overview

The Internet can be used to find information on nearly anything—from why the sky is blue to how to meet someone interested in your favorite movie. However, FINDING the information you seek can be frustrating. Which search engine should you use? How do search engines find and return results? How can you narrow your search so you aren't getting bogus results? What is the easiest way to make your searches more effective?

Goals: The goals are for you to (a) understand the basics of how different search engines work and (b) understand how to conduct effective searches.

Vocabulary

Familiarize yourself with the following terms. Refer to this section throughout this lesson as you work through the activities.

- **Address bar:** The address bar can be found at the top of any webpage (unless you have your preferences set to hide the address bar). Each Internet site has its own unique address. This address has two representations—a numerical one and a "name." For example, i-SAFE's Web address is www.isafe.org.
- **Domain name:** Domain name refers to the "name" used for a Web site, such as isafe.org. It can consist of alphanumeric characters separated by periods and directs the browser to a specific address on the Web.
- **Hits:** The Web site links resulting from an online search.
- **Search engine:** A Web site that allows you to search online for the information you want. Search engines use different methods to conduct searches.
- **Web browser:** A program that allows you to look at information on the World Wide Web or Internet. Common Web browsers include Internet Explorer, Firefox, and Safari.

Talk About It

- Do you know any specific domain names/addresses for sites that you frequently use?
- Do you use the address bar to locate common/frequently used sites?
- If you do not use the address bar, why not?

Section 2

Free Write

It is important to understand why you commonly use search engines. Do you typically conduct research? Do you look for Web sites of specific companies/organizations?

Describe various experiences you have had conducting searches online. What frustrates you in conducting online searches? What have you found to make it easier to locate what you are looking for?

_____

_____

_____

_____

_____

_____

Section 3

Think About It

One of the best things about the Internet is the ability to find information on just about any subject you can think of. However, Internet information isn't all in one place or divided into sections, like your local library. Therefore, there is a need for a way to search the wide variety of content to get exactly what you are looking for.

Think about it; searching for anything can be frustrating. You need somewhere to start, an idea of what you are looking for, and the tools to find it. Searching on the Internet works the same way. You need to understand something about the different search tools and techniques.

In general, search engines work by allowing you to type in keywords, phrases, and eliminators to define your search. The search engine then finds information based on what you enter and presents that information to you in a list of links or "hits." Some search engines return lists of links, and others offer summaries of the links. However, how the engines find that information can differ. How each engine interprets your "request" or your "search string" can differ also.

It is important to remember that search engines are NOT standardized. Each works in its own way. Through practice and reading up on your favorite search engines, you will be able to learn how to fine-tune your search queries.

Think About It—How Search Engines Work

Search engines work in different ways. In general, they use one of three common ways:

- Spidering
- Human-submitted
- A combination of the above

Spidering: Spidering is a name for a computer robotic program that visits Web sites, reads the information on the site, the site's meta tags, connected links, and other information to build its cache of links for various search terms.

Loosely defined, spidering is based on a computer program that retrieves documents, files, or data from a database or from a computer network. Another name for these programs is "crawlers." In general, these programs fall into three main categories:

- **Metasearch:** Metasearch engines identify key words listed on a Web site and match them to your search term or phrase. AltaVista was one of the first metasearch engines.
- **Full-text index:** Full-text index, as the name implies, records all text and returns results in order of how often your term or phrase appears. Google is a good example of a full-text index.
- **Topic/subject directories:** A topic/subject directory is like an encyclopedia in which each topic/subject is defined in a section. Wikipedia.org is a well-known topic/subject directory.

Human-submitted: Human-submitted search engines depend on owners/creators of Web sites to submit overviews of the sites and/or editors to review sites for content.

Combination: Some search engines use a combination of both methods. They allow spiders to collect results and then have editors/reviewers review content of sites and rate sites for use.

Important note: Some search engines also work from advertisements/paid funding. In other words, the site that tops the return may have paid money for that position. Along the same lines, some sites pay money to increase their visibility to spidering programs. This is an option for you if you have a service or product you want to have good visibility through the searches of others.

Section 4

Activity

Directions: Do your own search. Write the names of other students who fit each characteristic listed below (or assign them numbers):

- Those wearing jeans.

_____

_____

- Those wearing jeans and a t-shirt.

_____

_____

- Those wearing jeans that are not blue.

_____

_____

- Those wearing t-shirts.

_____

_____

- Those wearing t-shirts that do not have logos or pictures.

_____

_____

- Those wearing earrings.

_____

_____

- Those wearing earrings or hair ornaments.

_____

_____

Which key words clued you in on how to select the names for each statement?

_____

_____

Think About It—How Search Terms Work

It is difficult to give advice on how to phrase search terms because nearly every search engine differs. Here are some common things to try when conducting searches. Remember, it is often helpful to conduct searches on multiple search engines because each one uses a different "formula" for returning results and may search different parts of the Internet. Also, as you become familiar with different search engines, you will be better able to refine and decide how to phrase search queries.

Boolean logic: Boolean logic is a system of symbolic logic for computers devised by British mathematician George Boole. Because the Internet is a huge computer database, people must search its contents according to the rules of computer database searching. Much database searching is based on the logical relationship among search terms, referred to as the "principles of Boolean logic." AND, OR, and NOT are the key terms used to differentiate in the search.

Activity Extension

Go back to the activity in the previous section. Identify the Boolean terms used.

- **Phrase searching:** Some search engines allow "phrase searching." To use this feature, use quotations around the specific phrase you are looking for. The engine should return ONLY items/documents that contain that specific phrase, rather than those unlinked words.
- **Multiple keywords:** In general, the more keywords you enter relevant to topic, the more likely the resulting article will be relevant.
- **Advanced search forms:** Some (but not all) search engines allow you to conduct "advanced" searches. These searches allow you to fill in a form in a guided manner answering questions, such as which words to exclude from your search, whether to search on some or all words, how many hits to return, whether to display a summary of returned links, and so forth. These forms are great for those who want to narrow results or don't know how to use other search engine tips such as Boolean logic.
- **+/– system:** Another system used by some search engines is a simple + and/or – system. To search for a keyword, include a plus sign. To exclude words from a query or to ensure they are not in the result, add a minus sign in front.

Remember, not all of the above are used by every search engine. Each search engine operates using its own search queries and programs for narrowing results. Through trial and error and some simple research on your engine of choice you can perfect your searching.

Go Online
Option 1

Go to your favorite search engine (google.com, about.com, yahoo.com, ask.com, or bing .com) or try different ones to find which suits you best.

Using the tips you've learned, try to find links that would be useful if you were researching the following:

- Why the sky is blue
- The five richest people in the United States
- The best dog breed to have around kids

Write down information you found useful in narrowing your search. What types of information helped narrow down links.

Option 2

Conduct a Web search to find the top search engines and how each one works; specifically, how to narrow searches, whether they accept Boolean terms, and so forth. List what you find for each search engine.

Activity

Self-Check

Complete the following "self-checks" relevant to the search concepts presented in this lesson.

❏ I know how to complete a phrase search to ensure more specific "hits."

❏ I am familiar with several different search engines.

Reaching Others

At Home

Do you have a younger brother or sister? Offer to help him or her conduct more effective searches by sharing what you have learned.

Lesson 2: Job Hunting Online

Section 1

Topic Overview

Job hunting has certainly evolved with the advent of the Internet. More and more companies are using online ads and online job search engines to advertise or find new employees. Learn more about how to job hunt online through both the big search engines and the smaller classified ads sources.

Goal: The goal is for you to understand how the Internet can facilitate your job search efforts.

Vocabulary

Familiarize yourself with the following terms. Refer to this section throughout this lesson as you work through the activities.

- **Craigslist:** Craigslist.org is a centralized network of online communities, featuring free online classified advertisements with sections devoted to jobs, classified sales, rentals, and more.
- **Headhunter:** A person who recruits personnel to fill job vacancies.
- **Networking:** The act of meeting new people in a business or social context.

Talk About It

Explore what you know about job hunting online:

- Have you ever found or pursued a job online?
- What job search engines are you familiar with?
- How has the online environment made job searching easier?

Section 2

Think About It

The Job Search

Typically, there are four stages to a job search:

- **Preparation:** Designing your resume, writing the cover letter, and laying the basic foundation for your job search.
- **The search:** Actually searching for a job.
- **Application:** Submitting applications for your job choices.
- **Post-hiring:** Suspending or maintaining the job search.

Preparation

1. Decide what you want to do. What area will you focus on? What career are you interested in? For help, you can conduct searches for career placement online. The resulting links can help you determine what you want to do. There will be quizzes and more to help you narrow down your interests.

   My Job Area of Interest:

   _____

2. Get comfortable with your computer and being online. A good portion of job searching can be conducted online. Try a few sample searches. Use Google or another search engine and type in the job area of interest you listed above, for example, "English teacher." Follow that with the term "jobs," such as "English teacher jobs." What do you come up with? Any useful sites or returns?

   _____

3. Research your selected career choice. Who are the major employers? What salary can you expect? Go online and search for the following information for your selected job category:

   - Salary range
   - Major employers
   - Required degrees/experience
   - Targeted search engines for this category?

   _____
   _____
   _____
   _____

4. Put together your resume, including an Internet version. For guidance and help, do a search for resumes for your career to find examples.

 ## Go Online

Search for a sample resume for your selected job. What did you find? Sample resumes can be a good starting point to see how to position your strengths for your selected job. However, don't just copy these resumes word for word. Insert some of your own creativity and personality to help make your resume stand out from others in the crowd!

Use the outline below of the common categories of an online resume when creating your own.

Contact Details

- Your first and last name
- Your address
- Cell/mobile phone number
- Home phone number (optional)
- E-mail address (your personal e-mail address, not your employer's)

Profile

- Create a profile on your resume as a quick outline of who you are and what you can do for your next employer.

Major Achievements

- Use four or five examples of your work and what this has meant for your present company. Did the company save money as a result of an innovative program you initiated, for example?

Career History

- Include job titles, company names, and the dates you worked for each company.

Education, Qualifications, and Training

- Your industry- and job-specific qualifications go in this section.

Optional Sections

- Language skills
- IT skills
- Personal details
- References

Go Online

Find a free e-mail hosting service. You can try gmail.com, yahoo.com, hotmail.com, or others. Sign up for a free e-mail account to use in job applications.

Don't use your old/current e-mail address because, among other things, applying for jobs can open you to spam, or your current employer might notice.

The Search

Some studies say there are as many as 80,000 Web job-search sites. You're going to want to narrow down to the ones most useful for you and your chosen career. Consider:

1. **The big search engines:** Some job-search engines are extremely comprehensive, with hundreds of thousands of listings. Look through these and see whether they cover your career choice. Selectively submit your resume.

2. **Job-specific search engines:** Many job/career choices have their own search engines. Want a job as a nurse? You can find a search engine specific to that. Want to find a job in the telecom field? Chances are you'll find an engine specific to that field also. Do some research and see whether the career you have chosen has a specific search engine(s). These can be great for networking also.

3. **Top employers:** Know who you want to work for? Have an idea of who the big employers are for your career choice. Visit their Web sites to gather information on the company, potential jobs, and more.

4. **Regional search engines:** Check out regional, county, or even state job search engines to find jobs specific to your locale.

5. **Headhunters/recruiters:** Visit headhunter sites and see what jobs they have to offer.

6. **Online classified ads:** Your local newspaper, craigslist.org, and other online ad databases are great resources for job hunters.

7. **Networking:** Remember, not all jobs are found online. In fact, getting the inside track for many jobs is all about networking with people you know.

Application

There is a variety of ways to submit a job application for a position found online:

- **Fill out the application online:** This may include an option to upload your cover letter and resume in a Word doc or text format.
- **E-mail your cover letter and resume:** This will require you to create a short introductory e-mail message. Pay attention to exact titles or job numbers that may need to be referenced in the subject line of your e-mail application.
- **Use the mail:** Mail print copies of the application to the prospective employer.

Tips

- Make sure as you apply and submit your resume for various companies that you tailor your cover letter and resume to each position.
- Fill out online applications carefully and thoroughly. Don't skip sections.
- Does the application ask for your Social Security number? Think carefully before giving it out on an application. You can always add it if you are considered for the position. However, do not leave the section blank; make a note that, for personal security reasons, you will provide not it unless considered for the job.

Managing Responses

- Responses to your online job applications will come via e-mail or phone call. Check your e-mail and voice mail regularly to ensure a prompt reply.
- Try to validate response e-mails as showing actual interest in you for a specific job position. Providing your resume online will sometimes generate e-mails from services that want you to pay them to find a job for you. Think before you respond. Is this a service you really need?

Post-Hiring

When you've been hired, close down your active searches and either remove or deactivate your resume on search engines.

Section 3
Job-Hunting Tips

1. **Think privacy first:** Post your resume wisely and decide carefully what contact information to include. What would your current employer think if he or she found your resume online?
2. **Diversify:** Don't use JUST the big-name Web job sites. Only a small selection of jobs can be found there.
3. **Don't blast your resume out to all the sites:** Be sure to customize it for the job you are applying for. Carefully select which jobs to apply for and make sure to follow up the resume with a phone call or e-mail.
4. **Don't apply for jobs while you are at work on your current job!** That is an inappropriate use of company assets. Save job hunting for your own time and computer (or use the library's).

5. **Cover all bases:** Be sure you're professional all the way around. Look carefully at things others might forget—such as your e-mail address—and don't use one like hotstuff@hotmail.com to apply for a job. Always proofread everything several times.

Think About It

Last, but not least: Do you have a MySpace page or other public social-networking web-page? Employers frequently search about prospective employees on these sites to find information regarding their lifestyles. Make sure you won't embarrass yourself. Review information on "digital footprints" found in Chapter 2 of this book to ensure information about you found online won't disqualify you for future job opportunities.

Go Online

1. Use the online search skills learned in the previous lesson to find an online job search service that you would be interested in using. List the steps required to sign up and search for jobs. List the optional features available on the site.

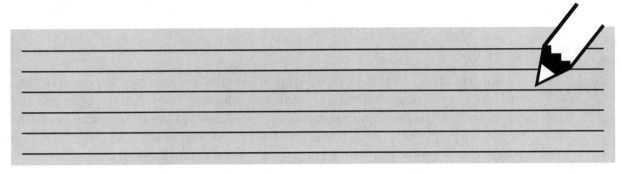

2. If applicable, go to your social-networking webpage and make sure it doesn't reveal personal information you would rather not have strangers or prospective employers know.

Lesson 3: Money Management with Technology

Section 1

Topic Overview

Before the age of technology, money management for most of us meant pen and paper and perhaps a calculator. Balancing and budgeting weren't much fun. Other money management items were practically unheard of, such as comparing loan rates or filing your taxes on your own. As for knowing your credit rating, that was unlikely. However, with technology, all of these money management tasks are made simple!

Goal: You will learn how the Internet can be used to simplify money management, as well as ways to access accounts and other financial items in a safe manner.

Vocabulary

- **Credit report:** A report containing detailed information on a person's credit history, including identifying information, credit accounts and loans, bankruptcies and late payments, and recent inquiries. It can be obtained by prospective lenders, with the borrower's permission, to determine his or her credit worthiness.
- **Credit score:** A numerical rating given in a credit report that indicates credit worthiness.
- **Credit worthiness:** An estimate of the amount of credit that can be extended to a company or person without undue risk.
- **Reconciliation:** The process of making compatible or consistent.

Talk About It

Explore what you know about money management online:

- Name some ways people can use the Internet to manage finances.
- Do you access your bank records online?
- Have you ever paid bills online? What were your experiences?

Think About It

With technology, managing your money has become much easier. Nearly every money management task can be accomplished with technology and going online, from balancing your budget, to applying for a loan, to checking your credit report, and even to paying bills.

Section 2

Credit Reports

Credit reports are now available online, usually at no cost. Use the search term "free credit report" to find links to central sites that allow you to request a free credit file disclosure, commonly called a credit report. These are available at no cost once every twelve months from each of the nationwide consumer credit reporting companies: Equifax, Experian, and TransUnion.

Each company can be accessed separately. The credit file disclosure, or credit report, provides you with any or all of the information in your credit file. This information is maintained by a consumer reporting company and can be provided to a third party, such as a lender. In addition, the disclosure will also include a record of anyone who has received a consumer report about you from the company within a certain period of time. The report will also include information that is NOT divulged in credit inquiries, such as inquiries of companies for pre-approved offers of credit or insurance and account reviews, along with any medical account information.

Pulling your credit report will allow you to verify that there is no fraudulent or illegal activity, such as credit cards you did not open. It will ensure all your aliases are correct, as well as your address, phone number, and more. Information for reporting errors will also be provided.

While credit reports are free online, if you wish to know your credit score, you will probably have to pay a small fee. A credit score is how a reporting company rates you. The higher your score, the better rates you can find on loans, credit cards, etc. It can be important to know your credit score.

(Optional) Go Online

Do an online search for a central service offering free credit reports from the three credit reporting companies. Try pulling your credit report from one of the three credit reporting companies. You will need to verify who you are by putting in your Social Security number and by answering a few questions to confirm your identity.

Tip: When filling in your Social Security number online DO NOT save the information to the webpage if asked in your browser.

What does your credit report look like?

_____

_____

Confirm that all the accounts listed on the report are yours. What have you learned about your credit report?

_____

_____

_____

_____

_____

Section 3

Loans

Interested in a loan for a car, school, or your first home? You can look for the best rate, apply, and even be approved online.

Advantages of Finding/Applying Online

- You can comparison shop loans.
- The Internet allows you to compare apples to apples, that is, you can ensure the loan terms are the same, see how the rates compare, etc.
- You can search/shop whenever you want, even in the middle of the night.
- You're not limited to a loan from one particular bank.

Disadvantages of Finding/Applying Online

- Some people may find the process impersonal.
- Some people are not comfortable using the Web. If necessary, you may ask for help from someone more Web-savvy to help you.
- Special circumstances may be more difficult to account for online. If you need a specific kind of loan or something tailor-made, you may be better off speaking to a human being.

What to Watch Out For

- Don't comparison shop just for fun. Each time you give an online lender your Social Security number the lender may do a credit check. Repeated credit checks can harm your credit rating.
- Try to keep credit requests within a fourteen-day window. Multiple requests during this period will be regarded as a single inquiry.
- Be careful, as always, about revealing personal information online. Ensure the site has a security policy and that your information will be protected.

Go Online

Take some time to see how easy comparison shopping for loans can be. Conduct a search to "compare loan rates." You should be able to get an idea of current loan rates for your area. Just remember, don't fill in any personal information unless you actually want to apply for a loan! What have you learned about shopping for loans online?

Section 4

Paying Bills Online

It is estimated that U.S. consumers pay approximately seventeen billion bills every year. Most Americans spend an average of two hours each month paying bills. With online technology, nearly any bill can be paid online.

Advantages of Paying Bills Online

- Saves on checks—each check typically costs a dime.
- Saves postage.
- Faster than old-fashioned bill payment.
- Secure and easy.
- Easy to track and export information to financial software.
- Can pay whenever or wherever you want—twenty-four hours a day, seven days a week.
- Less chance for late fees.
- You can schedule when you want bills to be paid and even set them up to be paid automatically each month.
- You can set up e-mail reminders.

Many companies allow you to pay online at their sites. Or, to make it even easier, set up bill payment through your bank. Most banks have an online bill payment system with detailed directions on how to set up and get started.

Safety in Paying Bills Online

Apply basic knowledge about security and safety in online communication to any online bill-paying transactions:

- Is the URL a secure one? Check to see that it begins with https:// (the s stands for **secure**).
- Make sure all financial activity online is done via a **secure** site.
- Does the site **encrypt** information that is sent? One way sites show this is with a small icon of a padlock or key during information transmission. It is often located in the lower right-hand corner of the page.
- Do not provide personal information, such as Social Security number, bank account number, credit card number, or any other financial information in an e-mail or IM request. No reputable financial institution would ask for this type of information in this way.
- Call the bank or company you are making payment to if you have any questions about its online security.
- Online transactions are not foolproof. Print out or electronically store confirmations of transactions.
- Cross-check your payments against your bank statements at the end of the month to make sure they match up.

See Chapter 1, Lesson 2, for more on staying safe when banking online.

Balancing a Checkbook

Balancing your checking account means matching the amount of money you say you have with the amount of money your financial institution says you have. This process is also called "reconciliation." Balancing your checkbook doesn't have to be a time-consuming task. Many budget management software programs are available. You can even find some free basic ones online by conducting a search for "free budgeting software."

These software programs allow you to put in recurring monthly bills, such as car payments and mortgages. You can even program periodic payments for things like insurance premiums or taxes. Then, as you track through the month, you can put in miscellaneous expenses.

One of the best parts of technology now is that you can easily log onto your bank account and compare your numbers with what the bank says! No waiting for that monthly statement.

Online Banking

Electronic banking has simplified banking. You can now review statements online whenever you want, cancel checks anyplace at any time, build your own saving plan, pay bills, and more!

Online banking makes sense in that it can save time and money. Having access to real-time account information can make a huge difference in budgeting. Additionally, online banking can help you spot possible account fraud activities earlier.

Section 5

Watch Out for Fraud

Managing your money online naturally requires attention to the possibility of online fraud and scams. Treat requests for money transfers or investment opportunities very cautiously. Refer to other lessons in this book to learn about specific online fraud activities and how to avoid risks.

Remember that, just as in the physical world, it is highly unlikely that anyone will offer money for free on the Internet. If it looks too good to be true, it's probably a scam! Manage your money online with caution and care.

Think About It

Think about online queries you may have seen or received via e-mail for investment opportunities or ways to make easy money online.

Lesson 4: Preparing and Filing Income Taxes Online

Section 1

Topic Overview

To some people, the thought of doing their own taxes brings on cold sweats and nightmares. For many, the IRS is the monster under the bed and, rather than take them on, they prefer to pay someone else to complete their forms. However, with the advent of technology, most tax forms are a snap! Additionally, the IRS has developed a free e-filing program to promote online filing for a large percentage of Americans.

Goal: To help you become familiar with how easy and safe it can be to file your taxes online.

Vocabulary

- **1098:** Documentation on mortgage interest statements and real estate taxes paid.
- **1099:** Form reporting income for those who are not employed directly by a given employer.
- **Adjusted gross income:** An individual's earnings for tax purposes, calculated by subtracting all allowable tax deductions from gross pay.
- **Audit:** A formal examination of an organization's or individual's accounts or financial situation.
- **Deduction:** A tax write-off or a reduction in the gross amount on which a tax is calculated.
- **Federal income tax:** Federal income tax is used by the government for managing and running the country. It is used for national defense, veterans, foreign affairs, social programs, physical, human, and community development, law enforcement, interest on the national debt, and more.
- **Gross pay:** The amount an employee earns.
- **Medicare tax:** This tax is used to provide medical benefits for certain individuals when they reach age sixty-five. Workers, retired workers, and the spouses of workers and retired workers are eligible to receive Medicare benefits.
- **Net pay (or take-home pay):** The amount an employee receives after all the taxes are taken out, along with any other deductions.
- **Social Security tax:** This is also known as FICA or the Federal Insurance Contributions Act. This tax provides for future retirement benefits, benefits for the dependents of retired workers, and benefits for the disabled and their dependents.
- **TRUSTe:** An independent, privately held organization that runs the world's largest Web privacy seal program.
- **W-2:** Form reporting earnings as an employee during a year.
- **W-4:** Form used to figure out the amount of income tax to have withheld from your paycheck.

Talk About It

Explore what you know about filing your taxes online:

- Have you ever filed your taxes online?
- Have you ever used tax filing software?
- Would you like to file your own taxes?
- What fears or concerns prevent you from filing your own taxes?

Section 2

Think About It

Understanding Your Taxes

The IRS requires tax returns to be filed by April 15 of each year. You can request an extension to the paperwork in writing, but must pay estimated taxes by April 15. The best way to prepare for filing your taxes is to save and categorize all of your records and deductions throughout the year so that you will be organized and ready when it's time to file.

Throughout the year, employers withhold payroll taxes and income taxes from their employees' pay. These amounts are sent to the federal government. Employees complete a form W-4 to help their employer determine how much income tax to withhold.

In general, there are three types of taxes withheld from a paycheck.

- Federal income taxes
- Medicare taxes
- Social Security taxes

Most states also have a state income tax.

Tax Preparation

Tax season begins each January and lasts until April 15th, the due date for filing. In general, employers are required to mail out W-2 forms, which report your income and deductions, to you by January 31. You might also receive forms from banks or savings institutions to report interest earned, investment income and 1098 forms for interest paid, and so on.

Activity

Before you begin to work on your taxes, be sure you have any and all information you will need. Look through this list and see which apply to you:

- Your Social Security number
- Birth dates and Social Security numbers for dependents being claimed on your return
- W-2s for all employment, including spouses if filing jointly
- All 1099 statements (could be 1099-DIV, 1099-R, etc.)
- Year-end investment statements
- 1098 mortgage interest statements and real estate taxes paid documentation
- Details on cash and non-cash charitable contributions you have made

- Self-employment income and expenses
- Documented unreimbursed job-related expenses
- Medical and health care expenses

Tax Preparation Software

Rather than paying someone to ask you questions and input answers into a software program, why not purchase a tax preparation software program that can easily walk you through preparing your taxes?

Be sure to pick the right software for your needs. Review the features of the programs. Do they have the features you need? Do the features save you time? Is there error-checking in the tax software? Is there a deduction finder?

Review the tax software navigation. Will you be able to move around your tax return without wasting time? What do the screen shots used for advertising show you?

Some benefits of some software programs include user-friendly features such as explanations of tax laws, instructions written in common language that are clear and understandable, and a guided interview to help you enter your tax data.

It is important that the program you select has a help and support feature. Is there a toll-free number you can call, an e-mail address, a chat feature, an online forum, or another way to find answers when you have questions? Does it only provide help for the software or also for tax-related questions? Some software programs even provide audit defense. If you are audited, they promise professional aid through the process.

Another feature you may want your tax program to include is state tax information. Will you need to purchase the state tax portion separately? How much will it cost? What if you have to file multiple state returns?

Finally, you will want to see how much the program will charge for electronic filing versus printing out and mailing in your tax return.

In general, tax software programs are divided into three categories: basic/standard, deluxe, and premiere. Basic software will walk you through a simple return, check for errors, and e-file for you. This software is typically best if you do not itemize deductions. Deluxe software offers more advanced help, including itemized deductions such as mortgages, charitable contributions, and other items. Premiere software is geared toward support for investments and small business deductions.

Once you install or download it (or access it online), be aware that the tax software will most likely need to be updated regularly. Tax software is often on the market even as tax laws are being released. So make sure you update your software before finalizing and filing. In general, experts recommend not filing before mid-February to ensure that tax forms are finalized.

Time-Saving Advantage

After you have prepared your taxes for the first time with tax preparation software, the next year it can be even easier! Information can be imported from the previous year's return.

Free Tax Filing

The federal government has developed a free federal tax preparation and electronic filing program for eligible taxpayers. Free File allows taxpayers with a certain adjusted gross income to e-file their federal tax returns for free. Typically, that means 70 percent of all taxpayers, approximately ninety-five million taxpayers, can take advantage of Free File.

Go Online

Go to the Internal Revenue Service's official Web site at www.irs.gov. In the search option, type in Free File. The IRS search engine will return articles related to filing for free. Read about "Free File."

- What do you now know about Free File?
- How does the site help you select a company?
- What are the benefits of choosing a company using the IRS site?

_____

_____

_____

_____

Section 3

Tax Filing Security

Is filing online completely secure? Double-check the site's privacy policy and make sure they are TRUSTe subscribers. Make sure that as you sign up you create a secure user name and password.
It is also wise to check the following:

- Go to File/Properties once you're logged in and click "Certificates." The security certificate should be current and owned by the company.
- Next, click on the "details" tab and look for the public key. Encryption strength should be at least 512 bits, but 1024 is better.
- On your end, make sure you have a firewall and your anti-virus software is up-to-date.

Final Note: The IRS notes that there are scams online. A taxpayer receives an e-mail notifying him or her of an IRS refund and directs the recipient to a site for more information. This site is phony and typically requests personal information, such as Social Security number. REMEMBER, never go to links in e-mails. Instead, go directly to the IRS site for more information.

Activity

Self-Check

Complete the following "self-check" relevant to the concepts presented in this lesson.

❑ I know how to access the official Web site sponsored by the Internal Revenue Service.

❑ I know what tax preparation software is used for.

Chapter 4: Other Online Considerations

> ## Chapter 4, Other Online Considerations, includes the following lessons:
>
> - Online Forms
> - Online Communication Basics
> - Working Wireless: Network Safety Considerations
> - Public Wireless Access Considerations

Understanding the Lesson Format

This chapter is designed to help you master a selection of basic online life skills. Each lesson is presented in sections to fully address the topic. Lesson sections include:

- **Topic Overview:** General description of the topic.

- **Vocabulary:** Critical terms and definitions used in the lesson.

- **Talk About It:** Provides thought-provoking questions. Depending on classroom setup, students can be directed to discuss with a partner, in a small group, or as a class.

- **Free Write:** Supports exploration of the topic through a writing prompt and space to jot down thoughts and previous knowledge.

- **Think About It:** Reference information and materials to consider specific to the topic.

- **Activity:** Each activity section includes directions to complete either a directed or worksheet activity to support learning.

- **Go Online:** This section provides an activity set up by the instructor to go online and apply what has been learned, either by researching a topic or completing a task.

- **Reaching Others:** This section provides guidance for extending what has been learned by sharing this information with others.

- **Self-Check:** A quick review to be sure you understand the concepts just presented.

Additional Resources

Your instructor may provide you with additional online and/or offline resources to complete these lessons.

Quiz

Your instructor may administer a chapter quiz upon completion of the lessons.

Lesson 1: Online Forms

Topic Overview

The Internet is a wonderful place to shop, play games, conduct research, and more. However, many sites ask you to provide personal information in order to create an online identity, confirm identity and age, help to customize preferences, and so on. This information is solicited via online forms. Online forms can make the online experience confusing. When is it OK to give out personal information? When should you not do so?

Goal: You will learn the risks associated with filling in online forms and how to determine whether an online form is safe and/or necessary.

Vocabulary

Familiarize yourself with the following terms. Refer to this section throughout this lesson as you work through the activities.

- **Cookies:** A small file that is sent to your computer when you browse certain Web sites. These files can then be accessed when you return to a site to help personalize your experience.
- **Form:** A document with blanks for the insertion of details or information.
- **Personal information:** Any information that identifies or describes an individual, such as name, citizenship, Social Security number, home address, and home telephone number.
- **Opt-in:** To choose to participate in something.
- **SKU:** A number associated with a particular product, often represented by a barcode. The SKU is used to track inventory and may or may not be shown to customers when they are shopping on the Web.

Talk About It

- Have you ever been asked for your name and other information in order to access a Web site?
- Where have you seen online forms used?
- What are some valid reasons for using online forms?

Think About It

We give away a lot of information online just by forgetting to click on privacy settings or by giving more information than we have to.

If you've ever entered your e-mail address online in a contest, submitted information to buy something, registered a product, or subscribed to an e-mail newsletter, you may have failed to uncheck an option in the fine print "to receive valuable offers from our marketing partners." In that case, you allow the owners of the Web site to sell or trade your address and the recipients to also sell or trade it, on and on down the line. In other words, you have "opted-in" to receive spam from solicitors you may never have heard of.

Perhaps of more concern is that you don't know how those "marketing partners" will treat your personal information. How will your information be used? Are they valid companies? Will they treat your information respectfully?

> **Best Advice:** Don't supply personal information without reading the Web site's license agreement and the privacy policy and without verifying the identity of the party requesting the information.

Security of Online Forms

Are online forms secure? Sometimes these forms can be digitally transported in a manner that leaves them vulnerable to undesired access. However, most reputable companies ensure their online forms are encrypted so only the intended recipients can access and read the information.

How information is stored and transferred is one of the keys to protecting a user's privacy. It is your responsibility to research the security methods a Web site uses to ensure that your personal information is kept private.

Go Online

If you are using an updated Web browser, it is designed to indicate whether the accessed page allows encrypted transfer. Typically, you will see a key or lock graphic in the corner of the browser screen. A broken key or open lock indicates an unsecured page. To learn more, click on the graphic and you can have access to additional security information about the page. As a general rule, don't submit information on unsecured webpages.

Can You Be Anonymous Online?

One common misconception is that you can be anonymous when online. Unfortunately, Web sites and software programs can keep detailed records about your browsing and shopping habits. For example, not long ago AOL went public with some of their customers' Web searches. The information provided to the public was surprisingly detailed and gave numerous clues to the users' identities.

Because of this, it is recommended that you avoid entering personal information, such as your name with Social Security or contact information, into a search engine on your own PC. Further, it can be wise to avoid using search engines run by your Internet service provider or e-mail provider who would be able to provide detailed information on you and your search habits.

Cookies

A cookie is a small file that is sent to your computer when you browse certain sites. These files can then be accessed when you return to a site to help personalize your experience. Think of it as the site assigning you a SKU number that contains detailed information that you have entered on the site. When you return, the site's server accesses your computer to read that SKU and customize your experience. For example, login, user name, passwords, shopping cart information, preferences, and other information can all be stored. Some sites even store information like credit card numbers in your SKU.

Cookies can simplify your online experience, but many are concerned that cookies intrude on their privacy. Carefully select which sites you allow cookies to be enabled for. Further, it is useful to periodically delete cookies from your computer. You can also go as far as disabling cookies in your Web browser.

Activity: Cookies

Delete your cookies. If you don't already know how to do this, open your Web browser and do a simple search for "deleting cookies in [insert your Web browser into the search query]."

Copy the instructions on how to delete cookies here:

_____

_____

_____

_____

_____

For example: In Internet Explorer, open the Web browser and go to "Tools." Then click on "Internet Options." Under the "General" tab you will see an option to delete cookies.

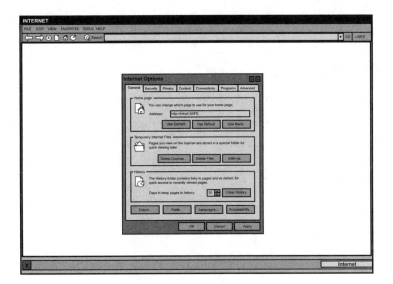

Activity: Setting Browser Security Options

Conduct a search for "Setting browser security options in [insert your browser name in the search query]."

What did you find out?

_____

_____

_____

_____

_____

In Internet Explorer, open the Web browser and go to "Tools." Then click on "Internet Options." Under the "Security" tab you will see different options to customize security settings.

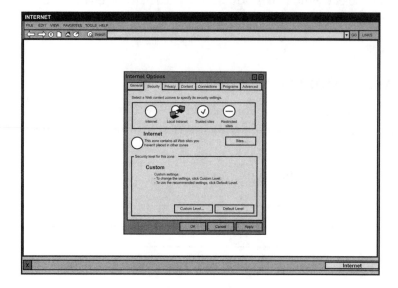

Forms in Pop-Ups or on Web Site Home Pages

One way Internet users are encouraged to provide personal information is on forms that pop up on Web sites or appear on webpages before you see actual page content. These types of forms may ask for your personal information, may ask you to fill out a survey, or ask you to enter contact information to collect a prize.

Activity: Pop-Ups

Complete this activity online or offline per your teacher's directions:

Think of types of Web sites that may ask users to fill out forms (real estate, game, school, or contest sites). Write four examples without going online OR go online and find four examples; write the URLs below and briefly describe the type of information the site is asking for. Then list what you think the personal information will be used for.

1. _____

2. _____

3. _____

4. _____

Apply It!

Apply what you have learned in this section. Think about the security of providing information to respond to these kinds of forms.

Write two tips that would be helpful to ensure that others do not endanger their personal information by responding to this type of advertising.

_____

_____

_____

_____

Basic Strategies: Selecting Anti-Virus and/or Anti-Adware Programs

After choosing the appropriate browser settings, an easy way to create a first line of defense in maintaining security for your personal information is to use an anti-virus program and/or a program that stops adware from collecting information about you. An anti-virus program can be set to automatically review Web sites as you visit them and alert you to possible unsafe or unwanted practices by the site.

Refer to Chapter 1, Taking Charge Online, for more information about anti-virus protection.

 Reaching Others

Home	Community
What safety precautions do you take at home? Are your parents, siblings, and friends also aware of what you have just learned regarding online forms, preventing issues, safety precautions, and more? How can you help those you know be safer and more secure online?	i-SAFE provides a variety of programs to reach others with Internet safety awareness and education. Are you in a position to provide community service by teaching youth, parents, or community members about Internet safety? Go to http://www .isafe.org to learn more about educator, youth, parent, and community programs.

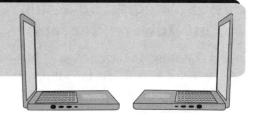

Lesson 2: Online Communication Basics

Topic Overview

Online communication—that's a breeze for you! Well, there's more to communicating online than meets the eye. There are many risks, dangers, and pitfalls to communicating online. Plus, there are numerous methods to communicate when online. We'll cover many of them and teach you what to watch out for.

Goal: You will discover how to participate in various means/methods of online communication in a safer and more secure manner.

Vocabulary

- **Chat:** Online chat can refer to any kind of communication over the Internet, but is primarily meant to refer to direct one-on-one chat or text-based group chat.
- **E-mail:** Electronic communication among users of a computer network.
- **Instant messaging:** Instant messaging is a form of real-time communication between two or more people based on typed text. The text is conveyed via devices connected over a network such as the Internet or cell.
- **Social networking:** A social network service focuses on building online communities of people who share interests and/or activities or who are interested in exploring the interests and activities of others.
- **World Wide Web:** Also known as the "Web," it is a system that lets you access information on the Internet. People often use the term Web to refer to the Internet, but they are not exactly the same thing. The World Wide Web operates over the Internet, and it is the most widely used part of the Internet.

Talk About It

Explore what you know about communicating online.
- What are some ways you communicate online?
- What are some drawbacks to online communication?
- How is online communication different from physical or face-to-face communication?
- What are some positive aspects of online communication?

Section 2

Activity

Directions: List Pros and Cons of communicating online below, giving your reasons.

Pros	Cons

Think About It—Research

Online communication happens in numerous ways. For example, reading information online is a fairly passive activity that can lull you into a stupor, minimizing your safety precautions. Unfortunately, people tend to believe what they read, see, and hear online. This can be a big issue when it comes to the Web, where nearly anyone can publish information—correct or not!

These days, it's difficult to do much research without using an Internet search engine. There are many great sites on the Web with useful information. You can find nearly anything you want. However, there are risks associated with searching the Internet.

Watch For

- **Inappropriate sites:** Unfortunately, the Web is full of information that many find inappropriate. From suggestive pictures to more hard-core nudity, these types of sites abound. And these aren't the only types of inappropriate sites to be found online. There are also numerous hate-filled sites and sites containing illegal and unethical advice, information, and more.
- **Faulty information sites:** Don't trust everything you read without double-checking the information for validity and checking references of the site for reliability. It is important to remember that anyone can setup a Web site and there is no requirement that the information posted be valid or reliable.
- **Private information:** Some sites ask you for private information before you can access them. Think carefully before filling out any forms. How can this information be used in ways you might not want it to?
- **Your own Web site:** Many people now have their own Web sites. You might want one too, but you do have to be careful about what information you display.

Think About It—E-mail

One of the most common tools for communication online is e-mail. E-mail is a great way to interact with others online, but it comes with its own pitfalls and annoyances.

- **Spamming:** Many companies advertise via e-mail. They try to entice you to purchase items, visit inappropriate sites, and so forth. Delete these e-mails. Do NOT click on any unsubscribe button found in these types of e-mails because this just confirms that your e-mail account is active.

- **Be careful when you reply to an e-mail:** You are including your e-mail address and you don't know where it will go from there.

- **Inappropriate, offensive, or angry e-mail:** Report these to your Internet provider.

- **The sender may not be someone you know:** Don't send personal information, photographs, or other information.

- **E-mail can't be retrieved:** Think carefully before you hit send. Don't write in a fit of anger or passion.

Think About It—Chat and IM

Chatting and instant messaging (IM) allow you to engage in real-time "conversations" with people around the world. In chat rooms, you type what you want to say, and then everyone can see it. Some chat rooms have specific interests, such as an actor or music group. Some chat rooms are moderated, which means there are people watching the conversation who step in to guide or enforce rules. Instant messaging works in a similar real-time format, but is a one-on-one interaction with another who is online at the same time. Typically, you can build a "buddy list" and your IM program will show you when those on your list are online so you can "ping" or send them messages.

Think About It—Social Networking

Social-networking sites, as well as traditional online forums, bulletin boards, and newsgroups, are all places on which you can read posted files, download or upload files, or post your own messages. Posted messages remain even after you leave. You can find an individual or a group on almost any topic and social networks are a great way to become involved in an area of interest.

Think Before You Post

- The biggest risk is including personal information in postings. Don't reveal anything that identifies you.

- Realize that by posting to some types of bulletin boards, you are making your e-mail address public.

- Groups that are illegal or want to spread hateful messages may try to involve you if you post contact information.

- Realize that anything you post online will be difficult to undo.

- Understand that many employers, recruiters, banks, police, and others are now searching online for information posted to social-networking sites. Don't post information you may not want to be public now, or even twenty years from now. This information DOES NOT go away. People have been known to lose jobs and be arrested for information they posted, even if that information was posted years ago.

Activity

Design a checklist for your online interactions based on the above information. Include the following, for example:

1. Is there a privacy policy?
2. Have you proofread your writing before posting?

_____

_____

_____

_____

_____

Issues Associated with Online Communities

Many issues that arise in online communities do so because of the following basic tenets of interaction in online communities.

1. **Online communities require you to provide personal information.** When you register for an online community, whether an e-mail list or a chat group, you are required to fill in certain basic personal information. At the most basic, this includes a user name, e-mail address, and password. However, more information is typically imparted as you interact in the community.

2. **Profiles.** Most online communities request, or even demand, profiles from users. These contain personal information that is available for other members, plus any others who care to search.

3. **Scams.** By participating in an online community, you are building a level of trust. You tend to reveal information as you become more trusting of the site. Participation in such a community opens you up to scams and spam.

4. **Permanent record of comments.** Comments online are, in essence, permanently recorded, despite the casual and familiar feel of some communities. Your information, such as children's names, workplace, vacation time, and so on is also being revealed to others. In addition, information about your health, finances, and personal life can be reviewed by others weeks, months, or years later.

Best Advice

Be Safe: Online stalking and harassment are rising trends. Use social-networking sites, but think carefully before adding buddies or social-networking friends you do not know in the physical world.

Lesson 3: Working Wireless: Network Safety Considerations

Topic Overview

More and more, technology is going wireless. Chances are that if you have multiple computers or a laptop at home, you've chosen to use a wireless network. However, going wireless at home brings up possible security and safety concerns.

Wireless, by nature, means that access to your computer resources and the Internet is occurring over the airwaves. Not only can the computers in your household access those digital signals, but so can anyone nearby. Basic safety and security precautions should be taken when setting up a home network and in maintaining the network.

Goal: You will learn the basics of setting up a safe and secure wireless network.

How Wireless Networks Are Set Up

Before the advent of wireless home networks, connections to the Internet had to go through a wire, such as a phone line or TV cable. Wireless networks make many things easier. For example, if you're cooking in the kitchen and need a recipe, it's now quite easy to use a notebook computer, connect wirelessly, and look up the recipe while keeping an eye on the stew.

Each computer that you wish to connect to a wireless home network must have a wireless network adapter, known as a NIC card or network interface card. These adapters contain a radio transmitter and receiver (transceiver) that allows the computer to send and receive messages, translate those messages, format information, and organize how the computer and network communicate.

Most home networks are set up so a wired connection comes into the house and connects to either an access point or a router that broadcasts the message out to those computers equipped with wireless network adapters.

Routers and access points are similar, with routers equipped with several other useful functions. Routers typically support Internet connection sharing and include firewall technology for improved network security.

Activity

If you have Internet access at home, think about the type of network that's set up. You may even be the one who set up the network at home. If so, do your parents understand how the network works? If Internet access fails on your network, how do you re-establish the connection?

Write those instructions here:

_____

_____

_____

_____

_____

Home Wireless Concerns

Wireless home networks have numerous features that make them beneficial. Setting up a wireless home network allows users freedom of movement without being connected to wires. It facilitates the sharing of information between computers. It allows computers to share one printer or access the Internet through one router. Who wouldn't like to be able to sit outside on a beautiful day and go online? However, there are some drawbacks.

Be Safe

What are the security risks and concerns associated with wireless home networks?

Think of it this way. Just as a radio station sends out a broadcast message that you are able to pick up with your radio—as is everyone else in range—so does your wireless router or access point. Granted, the range is much smaller, but chances are the signal can be picked up outside of your home by your neighbors or anyone else who happens to pass by.

Why should you care? You should have several concerns about anyone else using your signal.

1. You or your family can be held liable for illegal activity. If your neighbor is illegally downloading music over your connection, you might be the one blamed!
2. Your network speed decreases the more activity there is on it.
3. Others on the "network" may be able to view files on your computer or spread harmful software.
4. With access, others can monitor which sites you visit, read your e-mail, intercept your user names and passwords, and more—and you may not realize it!
5. A hacker could conduct a "denial of service" (DOS) attack. This is where noise or interference is introduced into the wireless network, causing devices to fail.

Obviously each of these dangers can be quite serious! However, with some forethought and planning you can implement protective measures to secure your wireless home network.

Protecting the Home Network

Unfortunately, most retail wireless products are sold with all security precautions turned off by default. Most people don't think twice about it because they set up the device, and it works for them. In fact, if you ever drive around in your neighborhood with a notebook computer with a wireless adapter, you might be surprised to see how many networks are open that you could jump on.

If you understands your home system better than your parents do, it's a good idea to help them go over the system. If someone other than you set up the system, familiarize yourself with your system and its settings.

The first suggestion is to read the manuals that come with your wireless products to see what security options are available and how to utilize them. Increased security comes with each of the following suggestions:

1. Set up or change the default settings on your router's Web-based administration. Most wireless routers can be managed online, allowing the administrator to refresh the router, monitor traffic, set passwords, and more. If you've never gone into the management of your router, chances are

a default name and password are used for access. That means anyone could go in and change your settings. For example, if someone detects your SSID with his or her computer and it has a default name of Linksys (the router manufacturer's name), the person will know some basic things. Linksys networks are set up at the factory with the default user name of "admin" and default password of "admin." So the person who detected your SSID can now log on and change those settings. To protect your settings and administration, you should go in and change the default user name, password, and SSID.

2. Set up encryption on your network. There are three basic types of encryption: WEP (Wireless Equivalent Privacy), WPA (Wireless Protected Access), and WPA2 (updated version of WPA). These encryption programs force users to enter a password which is encrypted before they can access the wireless network.

3. Most routers are automatically set to broadcast your SSID. The SSID is the Service Set Identifier. This is a broadcast message to every device within range of your network's presence. With SSID set to broadcast, anyone nearby can see the signal sent out by your network.

4. For really secure protection, you can even further restrict access to the network by allowing access to only "identified" machines. How does this work? Each computer has a MAC address (Machine Access Code), a unique number that every network-enabled device can be identified by. You can go into your router settings (managed through the Web-based administration mentioned above) and allow access to only those computers or devices you have entered the MAC address for.

5. A firewall is another item that can help protect any devices connected to the network. Also be sure to run anti-spyware and anti-virus software. For more information on this, conduct a search or refer to Chapter 1.

Additionally, use basic common sense and caution. Don't store files on your computers that contain lists of passwords, financial information, and so forth. If your network is ever broached, these files could be accessed (also, if anyone ever stole your computer he or she would have access to this information!).

> Remember, nothing is ever 100 percent secure. However, chances are that if hackers or criminals face resistance, they'll move along to an easier victim who isn't so careful.

Activity

Run through the following checklist to see whether your network is as protected as it could be. Read your manual or conduct an online search for instructions about setting security options on your network devices.

- Change the default settings on the Web-based administration.
- Set up network encryption.
- Disable the auto SSID broadcast.
- Set up a list of acceptable MAC addresses in your Web-based administration.
- Set up firewalls on all devices.
- Run anti-virus software on all devices (and update frequently).
- Run anti-spyware software on all devices.
- Ensure no passwords or sensitive financial information is stored in files on your computer.

Reaching Others

Do you know others who have home wireless networks set up? Perhaps they would also benefit from this type of information. Don't be afraid to share.

Lesson 4: Public Wireless Access Considerations

Think About It

With a laptop computer and a wireless network adapter, you can connect anywhere there is an open wireless network. This includes public places that advertise wireless access, such as coffee shops, airports, hotels, and other spaces. We've already discussed the security risks associated with home wireless networks. What are the risks of using a public network?

Goal: To consider how technology advances, such as public wireless access points, impact safety and security considerations.

Things to Consider

Public networks are just that—PUBLIC. That means you're not the only one online and others could intercept messages you are sending.

Take this into consideration when you choose to use these types of networks. You don't want to conduct certain types of business on them. For example, don't choose to purchase that book from Amazon when sitting at the network café. You'll be broadcasting your credit card number. And, although it's tempting to check your e-mail while sitting at the airport, you really shouldn't broadcast your screen name and password.

Besides thinking before browsing, here are some other security precautions you should take when using public networks:

1. **Use a firewall.** Make sure your laptop has a firewall installed and running. This will keep others from accessing your computer over the network.
2. **Read the privacy statement.** Public networks set their own encryption. Before using any service, read the privacy statement on the network's Web site to learn what type of encryption they use or whether they encrypt. If a network does not have a privacy statement, you probably should not use it.
3. **Hide your files.** If you have sensitive information on your computer, consider investing in software or updating your operating system so that you have tools to protect your information. For example, Windows XP Professional allows one to encrypt files on the computer very easily.

> **Important**
>
> When you are not actively using your wireless connection on your computer, TURN IT OFF! Make sure when you are using your computer in public, but NOT sending e-mail or surfing the Net, that you disable your wireless connection. Many public networks auto connect if you leave your wireless on.

Activity

Learn how to disable your wireless connection. Depending on how up-to-date your computer is, you may have several options. If you're using an external card, you can disable and remove it. If using an internal card, right-click the connection (usually located in the lower right-hand corner near the time) and select "disable." You can turn it on again when you need it.

Think About It

In some parts of the country, whole towns or areas of cities are "going wireless." Think about the impact, both negative and positive, this trend may have on society as a whole. Write your thoughts on how the following are being or will be affected by widespread wireless Internet access:

- **Advertising:**

_____

_____

_____

_____

_____

- **Business (for example, the coffee shop that provides wireless access):**

_____

_____

_____

_____

_____

- **Contact with friends and family:**

_____

_____

_____

_____

_____

- **Crime:**

_____

_____

_____

_____

_____

Free Write

Where do we go from here?

Widespread Internet access changes how we live and conduct our daily lives. Brainstorm a way that safety considerations can be incorporated into technology development to offset potential negative impacts of these trends.

_____

_____

_____

_____

_____

_____

_____

_____

_____

Chapter 5: Using the Internet to Move Forward

Chapter 5, Using the Internet to Move Forward, includes the following lessons:

- What Do I Want to Be?
- Further Schooling
- Online Education: A Newer Option
- Applications, Scholarships, Loans, Grants, and More

Understanding the Lesson Format

This chapter is designed to help you master a selection of basic online life skills. Each lesson is presented in sections to fully address the topic. Lesson sections include:

- **Topic Overview:** General description of the topic.

- **Vocabulary:** Critical terms and definitions used in the lesson.

- **Talk About It:** Provides thought-provoking questions. Depending on classroom setup, students can be directed to discuss with a partner, in a small group, or as a class.

- **Free Write:** Supports exploration of the topic through a writing prompt and space to jot down thoughts and previous knowledge.

- **Think About It:** Reference information and materials to consider specific to the topic.

- **Activity:** Each activity section includes directions to complete either a directed or worksheet activity to support learning.

- **Go Online:** This section provides an activity set up by the instructor to go online and apply what has been learned, either by researching a topic or completing a task.

- **Reaching Others:** This section provides guidance for extending what has been learned by sharing this information with others.

Additional Resources

Your instructor may provide you with additional online and/or offline resources to complete these lessons.

Quiz

Your instructor may administer a chapter quiz upon completion of the lessons.

Lesson 1: What Do I Want to Be?

Topic Overview

High school is nearly over and you have to figure out where you want the rest of your life to take you. This chapter is a step-by-step guide to help you figure out where you are going and how to get there. This first section starts at the beginning with determining what you want to do with the rest of your life. What do you hope to do to support yourself?

Goal: You will focus on the next phase of your life and how the Internet can help you achieve your goals.

Talk About It

As a child you probably dreamed about what you wanted to be when you grew up. A policeman, doctor, even an astronaut, all seemed so easy to attain. Now, however, there is a lot more riding on those decisions. What you want to be will affect what you do when you graduate, whether you go to college, what college you should choose, financial aid options, and more. That's a whole lot of pressure resting on that first question: What will I be when I grow up?

- What jobs are you interested in?
- Have you considered what you will need to do to get the job you want?

Think About It

Selecting a career you can picture yourself in is a big step. It's such a big step that many avoid thinking about it. However, it is the first step in planning what you will do after high school. It can determine whether you need further schooling, what schools you go to, and more.

> So how do you pick a future career? First, it's important to figure out a potential future that will make you happy.

Step 1—Know Yourself

Consider interests, hobbies, special skills, personality traits, extracurricular activities, and subjects in which you excel.

Example: Do you enjoy performing in the theater, can you write, do you prefer to illustrate, are you happy solving complicated math problems, or do you prefer to be out working in the yard?

List three to five activities you like to do or strengths you have below:

1. _____
2. _____
3. _____
4. _____
5. _____

Go Online

Select an online aptitude test that will ask you a series of questions to pinpoint your interests, strengths, and correlating career options.

Write in the results from online aptitude tests below:

_____

_____

_____

Step 2—Career Correlations

What career options align themselves to your interests and strengths?

Example: If you like to analyze how things work, you might like a job in research and development. Do you prefer to volunteer and help others? Look at entering fields such as social work, nursing, and so forth.

Select two of your activities or strengths and brainstorm correlating careers.

Brainstorming Chart

Strength	Possible Career
Strength 1	
Strength 2	

Step 3—Research

There are literally *thousands* of job options in our world today. Narrowing it down will depend on your interests. Once you have narrowed your options down, explore those to see whether any is your dream job.

Go Online

Directions: Select a career of interest to research, for example: Teaching.

1. Are there online networks for your job? If so, explore them and see what others have to say.

_____

_____

_____

2. What are the job options? Do some sample job searches.

_____

_____

_____

3. What is the pay scale? Schooling needed? Are there other considerations?

_____

_____

Offline Research

1. Attend an industry forum or trade show.
2. Interview or shadow an individual in the area you are considering. There is no better way for learning what is involved than by experiencing it or hearing about it first-hand.

Free Write

From your online and offline research what have you learned about the career you are interested in? Do you still think it is a good fit? Why or why not?

_____

_____

_____

Wrap Up

Making a decision is an important first step in moving on with the next phase of your life. However, keep in mind that most people today will change careers between five and eight times over the course of their working lives.

> With that in mind, make a decision that seems best based on careful planning and research!

Lesson 2: Further Schooling

Topic Overview

You've either selected a few careers you are interested in or know for certain what career goal you want to pursue. Does the career you have chosen include further schooling such as college or trade school? How do you know what you need and where to go for more schooling?

Goal: You will learn how the Internet can assist you in pursuing further schooling.

Talk About It

- Schooling is an important step for many in pursuit of their job goals. Considering your top job choices, what schooling will they involve?

Think About It

High school is an important time for parents and students. They may feel the end to schooling is just around the corner, but it actually is a time for new beginnings. Many jobs involve further schooling or, specifically, college. Selecting the right college is an important step in career planning.

RESEARCH, SELECT, and APPLY

Choosing a college is an important first step for the rest of your life. It is a tough decision that some make based on location, party stats, and so forth, rather than fully considering how it will affect their life goals.

So what do you need to know in order to pick the right college?

1. Start with your selected career.
2. What degree does that career require? If you are unsure, go online and do some research.
3. What schools offer that degree/specialization?

1. _____
2. _____
3. _____
4. _____
5. _____

4. Picture your ideal school setting. Circle your choices:
   a. Small school or large school
   b. Rural or urban
   c. Public or private

d. Other interests: What other things would you like your selected school to support? (Sports team? Extracurricular activities?)

1. _____
2. _____
3. _____
4. _____
5. _____

Go Online

Go online and, using the information you have figured out, start considering your school options and choices. What schools meet your requirements? Do you have a favorite? Rank your top three below:

1. _____
2. _____
3. _____

Applying

College applications can be overwhelming.

What to Consider

- Many colleges now have online applications.
- Research what you must do for the application. Do you need to take the SAT or ACT? Write an essay?
- Take the tests early. If there are issues or problems, you can retake it, but only if you plan ahead.
- What are the deadlines? Is there an early application window?

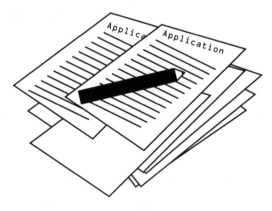

Wrap Up

Apply to your top three choices, along with a few others. Make sure you have options in case you are not admitted to your first choice of college. Before making a final decision, visit those schools that have accepted you and see whether you like the campus and the students you meet.

Lesson 3: Online Education: A Newer Option

Topic Overview

Online education is not a fad or a passing fancy. More and more accredited colleges are adding online or distance education programs. This lesson takes a look at the various levels of online education, its potential benefits and drawbacks, and how you can learn more about different programs. Finally, we'll deal with how to select an online university, if that is an option you choose.

Goal: You will learn whether online or distance education programs are an appropriate choice for you and how to select a university, if you so choose.

Talk About It

- Would you enjoy enrolling in an online education program?
- What are some benefits you can see for an online program? Drawbacks?
- Do you see online education as the way to go in the future?

Section 1

Topic Overview

Distance education/distance learning is a field of education in which technology (defined as print, radio, television, computers, and so forth) is used to deliver education to students who are not physically on site to receive their education. Some programs offer a type of hybrid program, requiring some physical on-site presence for portions of the course.

Today's distance education programs are increasingly relying on a virtual learning environment in which learning occurs via online chats, e-mail, virtual lectures, and other electronic media.

Benefits of Distance Education

There are numerous benefits to offering educational opportunities online.

1. **Availability:** The online environment brings the feasibility of taking unique courses to nearly everyone. No longer is a learner limited by distance or choices at the nearest college or course center. Now a learner can find courses online to fit any interest. Want to learn more about photography? Sign up. Interested in underwater biology? There's a course for you.

2. **Accessibility:** Taking classes online allows you to access course materials whenever and wherever you have access to a computer. If you only have time in the middle of the night or prefer to be comfy and cozy in your pajamas, online courses may be for you.

3. **Convenience:** Along with availability and accessibility, convenience is a top benefit of online education. By participating in online education, you can take courses when needed and as needed to fit your own schedule, rather than being restricted by the college's schedule.

4. **Cost:** Many times online courses are cheaper than traditional college and trade courses. Plus, costs for driving, housing, and meal plans associated with typical colleges are eliminated.

5. **Flexibility:** Online courses are all about flexibility. Typically, there is no set class time, and you may be able to choose when to complete assignments as they fit into your schedule. Further, some courses allow you to set the pace or even set your own degree plan.

6. **Learner Fit:** Online courses can be better for some learners who are visually motivated or learn best from experiential exercises. Also, the flexibility of an online environment can help those who may need more time, are language challenged, have a learning disability, are introverted, or have other issues.

7. **Non-Interrupting:** Online courses don't need to interrupt your daily life. Instead, you can select them to fit into your job/career schedule.

8. **Self-Directed:** Learners can direct their own learning experience and often focus on what interests them most.

9. **Time Spent:** With online learning little time is wasted; there is no drive time and no sit and wait time. Instead, time is spent logging on and learning.

However, there are some drawbacks to distance education.

Drawbacks of Distance Education

1. **Lack of Face Time:** With distance education there is little or no face time with your instructor and classmates. This tends to lead to less personalized attention.

2. **Lack of Social Interaction:** Online courses promote online interaction such as e-mail, chat, and discussion groups. This might be fine for many people, but others miss the chance to hang out with classmates and discuss assignments in person.

3. **Less Support:** The online course environment is more isolated. Students must find their own resources and learn more on their own. This might empower some, but it's overwhelming for others. The best way to overcome this is to make online connections, for example, find an e-mail buddy in the class.

4. **Making Time:** If you are a procrastinator or one who doesn't do well with setting deadlines, then online courses may not be for you. The very flexibility of the schedule can cause you to put off doing coursework or completing lessons.

5. **No Campus Atmosphere:** There is nothing to compare with that on-campus atmosphere. The college spirit, the beautiful campus, the extracurricular activities are lacking with an online course.

6. **Reputation/Perception:** While more and more mainstream colleges and learning institutions are offering online courses, many people still perceive them as the "easy way out" or not "real" courses. A stigma is still attached to online education, although this is fading.

7. **Technology:** If you're not computer savvy or not willing to learn new technology, then online courses will not work for you.

Activity

If you could enroll in an online class, what courses would you be interested in taking? Think outside the box and don't just list basic school courses. There are courses to design webpages and courses on photography, among others. What are you interested in?

1. _____
2. _____
3. _____

Go Online

Take time to go online and see whether anyone offers online courses in your interest areas. What did you find?

Think About It

One of the biggest opportunities for online education is in the college/university sphere. More and more colleges and universities are offering some courses online, and some have even offered entire degree programs online. How do you find one for yourself? What should you look for? Is it for you? Those are all things to consider.

Talk About It

There are many pros and cons to online education, as you have learned. Online universities are a growing arena in the education field. Many universities offer an online component to their traditional on-site classes. Other universities operate nearly completely online.

- Would such an option appeal to you?
- Why or why not?

Section 2

Think About It

Selecting where you want to go to college is a huge decision to make in itself. Add in the possibility of taking online courses to work toward a degree or to get started, and you have even more things to think over. The next section lists some items to consider in choosing an online college program.

Go Online

Pick a famous online college for practice in locating the following information. Some colleges known for their distance learning programs include University of Phoenix, DeVry University, and Kaplan University.

1. **Accreditation:** One of the most important things to consider as you look at online college courses and degrees is whether the university offering the courses is accredited. Regional accreditation is the highest form of accreditation in the United States. This ensures that the individual courses and general education you will be receiving have met established standards such as quality curriculum, governance, faculty, student services, and financial stability. Further, accreditation determines a school's eligibility for participation in federal (Title IV) and state financial aid programs. Proper accreditation is also important for the acceptance and transfer

of college credit, and is a prerequisite for many graduate programs. There are six recognized regional accreditation associations in the United States, and although each is independent, they recognize each other's accreditation. The following are the six associations:

The Middle States Association of Colleges and Schools: Accreditation of colleges in the middle states region (Delaware, District of Columbia, Maryland, New Jersey, New York, Pennsylvania, Puerto Rico).

The New England Association of Schools and Colleges: Accreditation of colleges in the New England region (Connecticut, Maine, Massachusetts, New Hampshire, Rhode Island, Vermont).

The North Central Association of Colleges and Schools: Accreditation of colleges in the north central region (Arkansas, Arizona, Colorado, Iowa, Illinois, Indiana, Kansas, Michigan, Minnesota, Missouri, North Dakota, Nebraska, Ohio, Oklahoma, New Mexico, South Dakota, Wisconsin, West Virginia, Wyoming).

The Northwest Association of Schools and Colleges: Accreditation of colleges in the northwest region (Alaska, Idaho, Utah, Montana, Nevada, Oregon, and Washington).

The Southern Association of Colleges and Schools: Accreditation of colleges in the southern region (Alabama, Florida, Georgia, Kentucky, Louisiana, Mississippi, North Carolina, South Carolina, Tennessee, Texas, Virginia).

The Western Association of Schools and Colleges: Accreditation of colleges in the western region (California, Hawaii, and the territories of Guam and American Samoa).

> It can be difficult to find a school's accreditation. One easy way is to visit the regional accrediting board's Web site and look up the institution by name.

What accreditations does the school you selected have?

_____

_____

_____

2. **Degree Programs Offered:** Once you have verified that the university you are interested in is accredited, take a closer look at the programs and curriculum offered. Do they align with your goals? Do they have the program and specialization you need for the job you would like? Specialization programs are important when considering large degree fields such as MBAs. Business administration is such a large field that the specialization options become just as important as the degree itself. Consider the courses the university offers. Are they all theory or do they involve practical application? Is the faculty composed of experts and experienced teachers? Are they available for help and guidance? Online teaching is different from in-class teaching; are the professors experienced in online teaching? Talk to the counselors at the institution and ensure that they will be available to help you and guide you.

For the university you selected, what degree programs are offered? Are any a match to your interests?

_____

_____

_____

3. **The Student Experience:** You've considered the institution and how it aligns to your goals; now you need to consider whether the student experience is one you can appreciate. An online

school does not have to be isolating and devoid of interaction. Will the university help cultivate a student experience that can make you better rounded as an individual? Is the school you're considering one that has an established learning community? Is group participation facilitated? Are professors and fellow students accessible for communication? Is the environment one that will challenge and grow you as a student?

For the university you selected, how is the student experience facilitated?

_____

_____

_____

4. **Support Services:** As for any schooling, there will come a time when you will need support from counselors, professors, or fellow students in making choices, understanding course material, completing the program, and more. It is important to learn beforehand what level of support is provided. Will you have an assigned academic advisor to help you select and navigate through your program? Are there online resources, such as a library or access to journals, for course support? Is support offered only at certain times or round-the-clock? It is important to have support so you do not feel isolated from the learning experience, from your professors, and from your peers. Will the university aid you in reaching your educational as well as your professional goals?

For the university you selected, what support services are offered?

_____

_____

_____

5. **Technical Requirements:** Not all online universities are created equally. Ease of access and delivery of content can vary from one university to the next. Before enrolling, consider how and when classes are accessed. How are assignments received? How do you communicate with professors and other students? What equipment do you need to access the course and participate? Is there technical support if you have difficulty accessing materials or posting assignments?

What technical requirements are there for the university you selected?

_____

_____

_____

6. **Cost:** Unfortunately, when selecting a university you must consider the cost of education and what financial aid options are available. Sometimes, online universities can be more expensive. The higher cost of online schools can be attributed to the need to hire experienced faculty and to pay for infrastructure and support services. You must weigh these costs against the convenience and flexibility an online environment provides. Think twice about any university with dramatically lower fees. Is it accredited? Is the support there?

What is the average cost of the university you selected?

_____

_____

_____

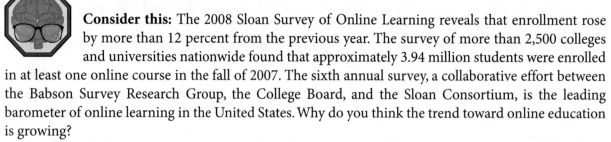

Think About It

Consider this: The 2008 Sloan Survey of Online Learning reveals that enrollment rose by more than 12 percent from the previous year. The survey of more than 2,500 colleges and universities nationwide found that approximately 3.94 million students were enrolled in at least one online course in the fall of 2007. The sixth annual survey, a collaborative effort between the Babson Survey Research Group, the College Board, and the Sloan Consortium, is the leading barometer of online learning in the United States. Why do you think the trend toward online education is growing?

Wrap Up

Selecting an online university is a big step. Make sure you are prepared for this type of environment and have fully researched your options.

Lesson 4: Applications, Scholarships, Loans, Grants, and More

Topic Overview

Just as education has gone online and high tech, so too have the resources to apply to those universities and for financial aid. As you prepare to go to college–whether a traditional four year, a community college or an online university—chances are you will be online to apply, find financial aid, locate loans, and more.

Talk About It

Wouldn't it be nice if college were free? If you could just select where you wanted to go and show up? Instead, filling out thick applications and writing essays, considering costs, filing tons of paperwork for government loans, and finding out what scholarships you qualify for can seem like a full-time job.

- What have you done so far to apply for college?

_____

_____

_____

Online Applications

Applying to colleges is now easier than ever in some ways. Universal online applications can be completed for a multitude of colleges. Even if your college doesn't participate in the universal application process, chances are they offer an online application.

Go Online

Select a college or university you have some interest in (Florida State University, Stanford, or Virginia Tech, for example) and see what their online application requirements are. Have you researched loans? Scholarships? Schools?

_____

_____

_____

Think About It

Many funding options are available for colleges.

Scholarships

Scholarships are financial awards based on merit, circumstances, or need. Think of applying for a scholarship as a contest. Typically, there are rules and regulations regarding who can apply. Some are restricted by ethnicity, others by parental occupation, some by what career you choose to pursue.

Searching for scholarships can be time-consuming and complicated. Start by asking your counselor for help, by asking your parents' employers, and by conducting Internet searches. Look for scholarships by your geographical location, by your hobbies and interests, and by your future occupation. Personalized scholarships with a smaller applicant pool will be easier to win than large national contests.

Scholarship applications will typically ask for information similar to what was on your college application: level in school, citizenship, state of residence, religion, ethnic background, disability, military status, employer, membership organizations, and so forth. Beyond these easier questions, be prepared to answer the following as well. (Write out your answers to the following questions and discuss them with your parents or teachers to practice.)

1. What are your talents and interests?

   _____

2. What subject do you plan to major in?

   _____

3. What career do you plan to pursue? Why?

   _____

4. Why do you deserve a scholarship?

   _____

Go Online

Conduct a few online searches to see what scholarships you can find that pertain to your interests.

1. _____
2. _____
3. _____

> Don't just depend on online searches. Ask at your library, counselor's office, Chamber of Commerce, and other places you can think of. You may learn of local scholarships that you have a better chance of winning.

When you are awarded a scholarship, keep in mind the following questions:

- Will the scholarship be renewed automatically?

   _____

- Is the scholarship dependent on maintaining a certain GPA?

   _____

- When is the money disbursed?

   _____

Grants

Grants are similar to scholarships in that the money does not need to be paid back. Grants can be awarded by the federal government, by a state government, by private businesses and organizations, or even by the institution you plan to attend. Sometimes grants are awarded in exchange for research work. The federal Pell Grant is one well-known grant awarded to undergraduate students.

Searching for grants is similar to searching for scholarships, and they are often lumped together because they need not be repaid. Ask at the university you plan to attend whether there are scholarships or grants you qualify for. Many universities and colleges are able to forgive portions of tuition or grant money to reduce what is owed based on either need or merit.

Loans

The school loan process is fairly simple if you follow the necessary steps. The first step is filling out a FASFA form. FASFA stands for the Federal Application for Student Financial Aid, the form that must be filled out to be eligible to receive aid from the government. The form asks simple questions such as what aid options students are considering. By filling out the form you will find out fairly quickly whether you qualify for government aid. However, there are other options as well.

You should also visit your local bank and see whether it has special offers for students who have been banking there. You can also use the Internet to search for various loan offers. Research is an important step in ensuring you find the best loan with the best rate.

Once you have loan options, sit down and run the numbers. Consider payment options and how you will use the money. After you have decided which loans to accept, the actual closing of the loan will be fairly simple. The last step in the process is contacting your school to confirm the loan money has been received. Ensuring they have received the money will help guarantee you aren't left high and dry when school begins.

Work Study

Work study is another way of funding your college experience. The work study program allows students to work part-time during the school year at the school as part of a financial aid package. The jobs are usually on campus, and the money earned is used to pay tuition or other college expenses.

Even if you aren't offered work study as part of your financial aid package, consider working part-time while in college to help with cash flow.

While it may be tempting to grab the money you are offered and run, consider the impact of paying back loans after graduation. Working to supplement financial aid can be a way of minimizing future financial burdens.

Important Reminders for Online Applications

1. **Prioritize:** List all of your activities and accomplishments and take time to prioritize which will have the biggest impact. Put those first!
2. **Be Diligent:** It can be tempting to treat online applications casually. Doing anything online can lead to carelessness because we are so used to dashing off quick e-mails and instant text messages with no concern for grammar or typos. Take the time to review your work. Before submitting your application, print out a copy, read it, and ask others to proofread it as well.
3. **Don't Leave Anything Blank:** White space on an application is NOT good. Consider adding more description to the things you are listing and dig deeply to make your application well rounded.
4. **Think Quality Not Just Quantity:** Rather than filling applications with miscellaneous information, personalize your applications and make them unique—showing a small sliver of your personality.

Chapter 1: Taking Charge Online

1. You are going to use a computer with Internet access for the first time. How would you make sure the computer will provide you with a safe and secure environment? Rank the importance of the following computer security measures from 1 to 4, with "1" being the most important measure.

    _____ Install and/or use spyware protection software.

    _____ Update the operating system (OS).

    _____ Use a firewall.

    _____ Install and/or use anti-virus software.

2. In simple terms, a firewall works by:

    a. Using filters to send you alert messages to avoid certain Web sites.

    b. Using filters to keep potentially harmful incoming packets of information from the Internet from getting through to your computer.

    c. Destroying e-mails from persons other than those in your address book.

    d. Providing a list of security software programs to install.

3. Spyware can do the following (select all that apply):

    _____ Monitor a user's Web activity.

    _____ Scan personal computer files.

    _____ Create pop-up ads.

    _____ Log keystrokes.

    _____ Change the default page on the user's Web browser.

    _____ Gather the user's credit card information.

4. One reason it is important to look for and read the privacy policy and "opt out" clause for an online bank is that online banks sometimes release information about your banking habits to other companies who want to sell you products.

    True   False

5. When you receive an e-mail from your online bank containing your PIN number or password, do the following:

    a. Write down the information and immediately delete the e-mail.

    b. Call the bank's customer service number to verify the information.

    c. Consider changing banks as reputable, secure online banks do not e-mail this type of information for security reasons.

    d. Forward the e-mail to anyone else on the account.

6. One of the first things to consider when evaluating a Web site is the home page's URL because:

    a. It always enables you to tell whether the information on the home page is credible.

    b. It ends with a code that gives a clue as to the nature or sponsor of the site.

    c. It must contain the name of the organization or company sponsor.

7. Which of the following items is a security consideration when evaluating a Web site:

    a. The author's name and qualifications are clearly listed on the home page.

    b. It contains true information that can be proven with a print source or other Web site.

    c. All links work.

    d. The user is not required to submit name and/or other personal information to view the site.

8. If an online task requires an exchange of money, it is important to make sure the transaction area of the site is secure. Which of the following designates a secure webpage?

    a. The URL begins with http://

    b. The URL begins with https://

    c. The URL ends in .sec

    d. The URL ends with an icon of a lock

9. It is not necessary to run your anti-spyware software after you shop on reliable, secure Web sites.

    True   False

10. You can prevent a malicious code attack on your computer by the following (select all that apply):

    a. Use a firewall.

    b. Use anti-spyware software.

    c. Run downloaded material through your anti-virus software before using.

    d. Use anti-virus software.

Chapter 2: Interacting Online

1. Which of the following is the best way to protect your personal Web site?

    a. Do not reveal your name.

    b. Do not post pictures.

    c. Password protect it.

    d. Blog only about work.

2. A password should be:

    a. The same for all sites you visit.

    b. A common word.

    c. Your birth date or other info.

    d. A random pairing of characters.

3. Which of the following can be used to help protect yourself on social networking sites?

    a. Filtering options.

    b. IP address logging.

    c. Anonymous post blocking.

    d. All of the above.

4. Which of the following safety tips applies to online gamers?

    a. Don't reveal personal information.

    b. Use voice masking if available.

    c. Don't reveal game site passwords to friends.

    d. All of the above.

5. Which of the following is NOT a means of communication that should be used in online relationships?

    a. Phone calls.

    b. E-mail.

    c. Instant messaging.

    d. Chat.

6. Online gaming bullies can be known as:

    a. Jellies.

    b. Griefers.

    c. Mangers.

    d. Fundits.

7. The MGM vs. Grokster ruling determined that:

   a. Illegal music downloaders could be sued.
   b. Software program designers/owners could be held liable for what users do with it, if the software promotes an illegal environment.
   c. That all P2P software should be shut down.
   d. That there are no legal uses of P2P software.

8. Which of the following are reasons P2P software can be dangerous?

   a. Malicious code.
   b. Inappropriate or illegal downloads.
   c. Spyware.
   d. All of the above.

9. Which of the following can occur when using P2P software?

   a. Illegal downloading.
   b. Legal downloading.
   c. Networking with others who share your interests.
   d. All of the above.

10. Providing identifying information on the Internet could potentially lead to which of the following?

   a. Problems with malicious code.
   b. Physical harm to family members.
   c. Both "a" and "b" above.

Chapter 3: Putting the Internet to Work for You

1. Which of the following is not a key search term used in Boolean logic searches?

   a. not

   b. and

   c. but

   d. or

2. A metasearch engine works by:

   a. Identifying words in an URL to a term or phrase in a search.

   b. Identifying the most popular Web sites on the Internet.

   c. Matching a search term or phrase to a list of Web sites that pay the search engine provider.

   d. Identifying key words listed on a Web site and matching them to search term or phrase.

3. When using a phrase search, one can search and retrieve only items/documents that contain a specific phrase by doing which of the following?

   a. Put the exact phrase in the search bar.

   b. Put parentheses around the exact phrase in the search bar.

   c. Put quotes around the exact phrase in the search bar.

   d. Put key words in the phrase.

4. Why is it recommended that you create a new personal e-mail account when searching for a job online?

   a. Applications may generate spam that you will not want in your original personal account.

   b. A different account makes it less likely that your name will be associated with online searches of applications.

   c. It is less likely that you will miss an application response e-mail.

   d. All of the above.

5. One of the great things about job hunting online is that one resume fits all. There is no need to customize for each job.

   True   False

6. In order to get "good exposure," it's a good idea to post your resume as often as you can on as many sites as you can, even if the sites don't necessarily list jobs in your field.

   True   False

7. Advantages of looking for a loan online include:

   a. You can comparison shop loans.

   b. You can search/shop whenever you want—even in the middle of night.

   c. You are not limited to a loan from one particular bank.

   d. All of the above.

8. A major disadvantage of having your credit checked repeatedly online is that:

   a. Repeated credit checks can lower your credit rating.

   b. The process will generate a lot of spam.

   c. Your bank will be immediately notified if your credit score is low.

   d. Online credit checks are not reliable.

9. One of the reasons tax preparation software is now so popular is that you do not have to keep paper records.

   True   False

10. An advantage of online banking is that it can help you spot possible account fraud activities earlier than when you use traditional banking.

    True   False

Chapter 4: Other Online Considerations

Each of the following situations depicts either an acceptable or a risky request for, or usage of, online sources and services. Select "Acceptable" for those that would pose little or no obvious threat to you. Select "Risky" for those that pose a threat.

1. You want to play free games online. You find a Web site through an online search. The home page provides no information about the site's content. Instead, you are asked to fill out a form to provide name, address, e-mail address, and phone number to enter the site.

   Acceptable   Risky

2. You are going to purchase software from a well-known company. In order to complete the transaction, you are sent to a URL that begins with "https" and are asked to fill out a form with billing and shipping information as well as a credit card number.

   Acceptable   Risky

3. You "Google" your name and Social Security number in order to find webpages that may contain this information.

   Acceptable   Risky

4. You want to join Facebook but are asked to fill out a profile before you can join.

   Acceptable   Risky

5. While waiting at an airport to catch a flight, you connect to the free, unsecured wireless network and log on to your online banking Web site to pay bills.

   Acceptable   Risky

6. The Johnson family is ready to create a home wireless network. They use the router and system supplied by their Internet service provider. It is complicated to set up a secured network and involves having the family remember passwords, so they leave it unsecured.

   Acceptable   Risky

7. The Kamdens live next door to the Johnsons (in 6 above). They realize they can sign on to the Johnson's home network for free and do so routinely to check e-mail, make online purchases, and participate in social networking sites.

   Acceptable   Risky

8. You receive an e-mail that indicates you've won a contest. You click on the link provided and are asked to fill out a form in order to receive your prize.

   Acceptable   Risky

9. You win an eBay auction from a seller who has a 98 percent positive user rating score and complete your purchase through PayPal.

   Acceptable   Risky

10. You want to download a new ringtone for your cell phone. An online search for "ringtones" takes you to a Web site that has nothing on it but a form asking for your cell phone number.

    Acceptable   Risky

Chapter 5: Using the Internet to Move Forward

1. How many times does the average person change jobs?

   a. 1 or 2
   b. 10
   c. 5 to 8
   d. Never

2. Which of the following is not a benefit of an online college.

   a. Accessibility
   b. Cost
   c. Convenience
   d. Socialization

3. The most important thing to look for in a college—online or offline—is:

   a. Accreditation
   b. Cost
   c. Location
   d. Degree options

4. It is important to research which of the following in selecting an online college.

   a. Accreditation
   b. Support services
   c. Technical requirements
   d. All of the above

5. Money that has to be repaid after college is called a:

   a. Scholarship
   b. Grant
   c. Loan
   d. None of the above

Chapter 1: Taking Charge Online

Lesson 1: Computer Security

Students are provided with two options:

Option 1

Visit http://www.microsoft.com/security/default.mspx and research computer security information. This site provides operating system updates, scans for malicious software, and no-cost anti-spyware removal tools.

Option 2

Do an online search for more information and/or resources about anti-virus software. List options and features that are available at no cost.

Teacher tip: To save time, prepare links of your choice for students instead of allowing independent searches.

Lesson 2: Online Banking

Students are provided with two options:

Option 1

Go online and conduct a search using the term "online banking demo." Select one of the sample demos that comes up as a search return and run through the demo to learn more about online banking.

Option 2

Go to an online banking demo that your instructor chooses and run through the demo to learn more about online banking.

Lesson 3: Online Research Skills

Student instructions: Take time now to evaluate a Web site. We suggest looking at your district or school Web site to gain some practice in Web site evaluation. Further practice can be gained evaluating Web sites your instructor directs you to.

Teacher tip: Select two or more Web sites for students to evaluate and compare for reliability.

Lesson 4: Online Retail Shopping

The Go Online section is optional.

Student instructions: Review an online shopping site selected by your instructor and rate it with your Web site evaluation tool.

Chapter 2: Interacting Online

Lesson 1: Your Online Persona

1. Students are directed to take some time to research ways and means to host a personal Web site. They are then to list the pros and cons of the various Web hosting services they find.

2. (Optional) Students are directed to obtain more information and options for sites that will provide free password protection code by using their favorite search engine to search a phrase such as "download free Web site password protection." The teacher may want to search this in advance in order to provide direct links to students (provided as a second option in the workbook).

Section 2: Digital Footprint

Students are directed to Google themselves and others to discover their digital footprints.

Lesson 2: Online Social Networking

Students are directed to visit a sampling of online social networks and browse around. They are then asked to answer the following questions:

- What safety and security risks do you notice?
- Do you see inappropriate pictures?
- Do you see inappropriate screen names?
- Do you see inappropriate blogs?

If you are not familiar with any social networking sites, find examples by doing an Internet search. Well-known examples include:

- Myspace.com
- Facebook.com
- Myyearbook.com
- Xanga.com

Lesson 4: Online Gaming

Students are directed to find Web sites that review gaming sites and offer feedback on online gaming.

Lesson 5: Peer-to-Peer (P2P) Networking

Students are instructed to go online and research the MGM vs. Grokster ruling by the U.S. Supreme Court and write short summaries of the ruling in their own words. The following summary from the U.S. Copyright office can be found at http://www.copyright.gov/docs/mgm/index.html and can be used to check student writings.

Supreme Court Rules in MGM vs. Grokster

On June 27, 2005, the Supreme Court issued its ruling in MGM vs. Grokster, ruling that the providers of software that is designed to enable "file-sharing" of copyrighted works may be held liable for the copyright infringement that takes place using that software. The Court held that "one who distributes a device with the object of promoting its use to infringe copyright, as shown by clear expression or other affirmative steps taken to foster infringement, is liable for the resulting acts of infringement by third parties."

Students are directed to go online to research the legal consequences of file sharing with regard to intellectual property concerns and copyright violation.

Chapter 3: Putting the Internet to Work for You

Lesson 1: Online Search Skills

Students are provided with two options:

Option 1

Go to your favorite search engine or choose one from this list: Google.com, bing.com, about.com, yahoo.com, ask.com, hotbot.com (or try different ones to find that suits you best).

Using the tips you've learned, try to find links that would be useful if you were researching the following:

- Why the sky is blue.
- The five richest people in the United States.
- The best dog to have around kids.

Option 2

Conduct a Web search to find the top search engines and how each one works, that is, how to narrow searches, whether they accept Boolean terms, etc. List what you find for each search engine.

Lesson 2: Job Hunting Online

Students are provided with two options:

Option 1

Use the online search skills learned in the previous lesson to search for an online job search service that you would be interested in using. List the steps required to sign up and search for jobs. List the optional features available on the site.

Option 2

Go to the online job search service selected by your teacher. List the steps required to sign up and search for jobs. List the optional features available on the site. In addition, fill out the following using online resources:

My Job Area of Interest: _____

Become comfortable with your computer and being online. A good portion of job searching can be conducted online. Try a few sample searches. Use Google or another search engine and type in your job area of interest as listed above, for example, "English teacher." Follow that with the term "jobs," such as "English teacher jobs." What do you come up with? Any useful sites or returns?

Research your selected career choice. Who are the major employers? What can you expect for a salary? Go online and search for the following information for your selected job category:

- Salary range
- Major employers
- Required degrees/experience
- Targeted search engines for this category

Put together your resume; include an Internet version. For guidance and help, do a search for resumes for your career to find examples.

Go Online

Type in your job interest sample resume. What do you find? Sample resumes can be a good starting point to see how to position your strengths for your selected job. However, don't just copy these resumes word-for-word. Call on some of your own creativity and personality to help make your resume stand out from others in the crowd!

Take time to fill in the outline below for the common categories of an online resume:

- Contact details:
  - Your first and last names
  - Your address
  - Cell/mobile phone number
  - Home phone number (optional)
  - E-mail address (your personal e-mail address, not your employer's)
- Profile: Use a profile on your resume as a quick outline of who you are and what you can do for your next employer.
- Major Achievements: Use four or five examples to outline your work and what this has meant for your company. For example, did you save money as a result of an innovative program you initiated?
- Career History: Include job titles, company names, and the dates you worked for each company.
- Education, Qualifications, and Training: Outline your industry and job-specific qualifications in this section.
- Optional Sections:
  - Language skills
  - IT skills
  - Personal details
  - References

Create a NEW personal e-mail account. Don't use your old/current one. Applying for jobs can open you to spam, your current employer might notice, etc. Many Web-based e-mails are free, such as mail.com, yahoo.com, and hotmail.com. They can also be anonymous.

Go Online

Find a free e-mail hosting service. You can try gmail.com, yahoo.com, etc. Sign up for a free e-mail account to use for job applications.

Lesson 3: Money Management with Technology

Optional Activity

Do an online search for a central service offering free credit reports from the three credit reporting companies. Try pulling your credit report from one of the three credit reporting companies. You will need to verify who you are by putting in your Social Security number and by answering a few questions to confirm your identity.

What does your credit report look like?

Confirm that all the accounts listed on the report are yours. What have you learned about your credit report?

Take some time to see how easy it can be to compare loans. Conduct a search to "compare loan rates."

Lesson 4: Preparing and Filing Income Taxes Online

Go Online

Go to the Internal Revenue Service's official Web site at www.irs.gov. In the search option, type in "Free File." The IRS search engine will return articles related to filing for free. Read about Free File.

- What do you now know about Free File?
- How does the site help you select a company?
- What are the benefits of choosing a company by using the IRS site?

Chapter 4: Other Online Considerations

Lesson 1: Online Forms

Go Online

Go online to see secure webpage symbols including a lock.

Activity (Optional)

Option to go online and find four samples of online forms.

Chapter 5: Using the Internet to Move Forward

Lesson 1: What Do I Want to Be?

Go Online

Take an online aptitude test. What are the results of the test?

Lesson 2: Further Schooling

Go Online

Consider college options by going online to research various campuses, what degrees are offered, and so forth. Select characteristics of an ideal school. Do some online research into schools.

Lesson 3: Online Education: A Newer Option

Go Online

What online courses could you take? Does anyone offer a class in your interest areas?

Pick a famous online college for practice in locating the following information. Some colleges known for their distance learning programs include University of Phoenix, DeVry University, and Kaplan University.

What accreditations does the university you selected have? What degree programs are offered? Do any match your interests?

For the university you selected, how is the student experience facilitated? What support services are offered? What technical requirements are there? What is the average cost of the university you selected?

Lesson 4: Applications, Scholarships, Loans, Grants, and More

Go Online

What scholarships can you find online that you qualify for?

Chapter 1: Taking Charge Online

Lesson 1: Section 2

Sample Free Write

I check e-mail regularly. However, Friday morning my e-mail box was full of messages. That morning I quickly scanned my e-mails. Hmm, besides the one from a friend I was expecting, another one catches my eye.

YOU ARE A WINNER!!! Wow—I wonder what I won!

I open the e-mail.

It appears to be from a computer game software site. It notifies me I've won a free copy of their newest game—Tektronic.

All I need to do is download the attached game from the e-mail and install.

I am super excited. I don't remember signing up for any contests, but hey a free game is super cool.

I click on the attachment and download it.

It takes a few minutes to download but then a menu pops up and asks if I want to install the program.

Of course I click yes!

And that is when things go wrong—really, really wrong.

My computer starts doing whacky things—e-mail pops up and sends for no reason at all.

A silly monkey pops up on his screen and does back flips while saying I GOT YOU!

And then, worst of all, the screen goes completely . . .

BLANK!!!!

Oh no! What have I done???

I try hitting keys and restarting the computer. No luck—the same stupid monkey and blank screen.

I forgot one of the critical rules in e-mail—ensuring the source of the content is valid and reliable before opening or downloading an attachment!

Lesson 3: Section 3

Online Research

Items in **bold** are possible student answers.

Ease of Use

- Is use of the Web site free of charge?
- **Does the page load quickly?**
- **Is the page layout easy to read?**
- **Do the links work?**
- **Are the directions about how to use the Web site easy to understand?**

Source

- Does the information appear to be true? Can it be backed up or proven with a print source or another Web site?
- Is it clear who is sponsoring the Web site?
- **Does the page contain information about the author's or sponsor's qualifications?**
- **Is the author's name listed on the page with a contact address or phone number?**
- **Is there a publication date, date of update, or both?**

Appropriateness and Safety

- Can you view the contents of the webpage without giving out personal information such as name, age, e-mail address, etc.?
- Is it clear why the sponsor is providing the site?
- **Is the site content appropriate for your age group?**
- **Can you understand the information/content?**
- **Is it free of advertising, or does it contain few advertisements?**

Lesson 4: Online Retail Shopping

Items in **bold** are possible student answers.

Ease of Use

- Is it easy to find information and what you are looking for?
- Can you find shipping costs?
- **Does the page load quickly?**
- **Is the page layout easy to read?**
- **Do the links work?**
- **Are the directions about how to use the site easy to understand?**

Reliability

- Is the site known to be reliable? (Why or why not?)
- Is there a feedback rating system or another judge of reliability?
- Does the feedback contain spaces for complaints as well as positive feedback?
- **Is there a physical store you know of that sponsors this online store?**
- **Are shipping policies and date of expected arrival clearly stated?**

Money

- Can you pay with credit card or other secure transaction method?
- Is a return policy posted?
- **Are shipping costs stated and reasonable?**
- **Are prices comparable to other sites?**

Quiz

1. Rank the importance of the following computer security measures from 1 to 4, with "1" being the most important measure.

   __4__ Install and/or use spyware protection software.

   __2__ Update the operating system (OS).

   __1__ Use a firewall.

   __3__ Install and/or use anti-virus software.

2. b

3. Spyware can do the following (select all that apply):

   __x__ monitor a user's Web activity

   __x__ scan personal computer files

   __x__ create pop-up ads

   __x__ log keystrokes

   __x__ change the default page on the user's Web browser

   __x__ gather the user's credit card information

4. TRUE

5. c

6. b

7. d

8. b

9. FALSE

10. a, c, and d

Chapter 2: Interacting Online

Section 2: Digital Footprint

Sample Answers

1. Things you do that leave digital footprints: blog posts, twitters, articles written and published, bulletin posts, etc.
2. Free Write: Why might someone care about his or her digital footprint? It is a written record for others, including future employers, college recruiters, friends, and associates, to view.

Cause and Effect

1. Janice posts a picture of herself drinking alcohol and making an obscene gesture on her social-networking page.

   Possible Effects/Consequences: Suspended from sports teams, future college recruiters notice, banned from honor club and other societies that reward personal responsibility, etc.

2. Mark posts his e-mail address in order to gain access to a dozen online gambling sites.

   Possible Effects/Consequences: Receives a lot of spam and inappropriate e-mails. Name associated with online gambling.

3. Morgan regularly bullies another girl via text messages, on blogs, and on her own personal Web site.

   Possible Effects/Consequences: Morgan is pursued legally and civilly for cyber bullying/harassment.

4. Matthew provides his art portfolio on his social-networking page. He regularly enters his digital art works in contests online and has won several awards. In addition to contest site recognition, five online articles have published the contest results that mention his awards.

   Possible Effects/Consequences: Matthew is recognized as an artist of merit, receives scholarships, attention, and opportunities. Colleges see his work and consider it in their selection process. It is beneficial when he applies for an art internship.

Quiz

1. c
2. d
3. d
4. d
5. a
6. b
7. b
8. d
9. d
10. c

Username:

Password:

Domain:

Chapter 3: Putting the Internet to Work for You

Quiz

1. c
2. d
3. c
4. d
5. False
6. False
7. d
8. a
9. False
10. True

Chapter 4: Other Online Considerations

Quiz

1. Risky

2. Acceptable

3. Acceptable

4. Acceptable

5. Risky

6. Risky

7. Risky

8. Risky

9. Acceptable

10. Risky

Section 2: Activity

Design a checklist for your online interactions based on the above information. For example:

1. Is there a privacy policy?
2. Have you proofread your writing before posting?
3. Is your post something you would feel comfortable with complete strangers seeing? Your pastor? A college recruiter? Your principal? Your parents?
4. Is your post likely to anger, intimidate, threaten, or make another feel uncomfortable?
5. Does your post contain questionable or objectionable material?
6. Could your post be considered risqué?
7. Does your post contain strong viewpoints, politics, or other material that you may not want to be associated with 5–10 years in the future?
8. Does your post contain information that could be used by others to discriminate (such as health information, etc.)?

Chapter 5: Using the Internet to Move Forward

Quiz

1. c
2. d
3. a
4. d
5. c

INDEX

Federal income taxes, defined, 77

File sharing, 55; defined, 54; program controls, adjusting, 55

Firewall, 3, 11; basics, 5–6; built-in, 6; hardware, 6; software, 6

Firewalls, and peer-to-peer (P2P) networking, 55

Flexibility, of online education, 106

Forms, *See* Online forms: defined, 83

Forums, 44

Full-text index, 63

G

Gaming online, vi, 49–53; cheesers, 51–52; creed, 52; danger of, 49; defined, 49; going online, 52; griefers, 49, 51–52; reaching others, 53; risks of, 50; safety tips, 51; self-check, 52; type of games, 50; vocabulary, 49

Go Online section summaries, 122–130

.gov, 17

Grants, 112–113

Griefers, 51–52; defined, 49

Gross pay, defined, 77

H

Harassment, 91

Hardware router, 6

Headhunter, defined, 67

Headhunters/recruiters, 69

Hits, defined, 77

Hosting, defined, 31

Human-submitted search engines, 63

I

i-SAFE i-PARENT program, 28

ILOVEYOU worm/Trojan horse, 7

IM screen name, posting, 34

Inappropriate e-mail, 90

Inappropriate sites, 89

Income taxes online, vii, 77–80; activity, 78–79; adjustable gross income, defined, 77; audit, defined, 77; deduction, defined, 77; Federal income taxes, defined, 77; Form 1098, defined, 77; Form 1099, defined, 77; going online, 80; gross pay, defined, 77; Internal Revenue Service Web site, 80; Medicare tax, defined, 77; net pay/take-home pay, defined, 77; security, 80; self-check, 80; Social Security tax (FICA), 77; tax preparation, 78; tax preparation software, 79; TRUSTe, defined, 77; understanding your taxes, 78; vocabulary, 77; W-2 form, defined, 77; W-4 form, defined, 77

Informational Web sites, 17

Instant messaging (IM), 44, 90; defined, 88

Intellectual property, 55

Interacting online, vi, 29; gaming online, 49–53; online persona, 31–39; peer-to-peer (P2P) networking, 54–58; relationships online, 43–48, 44–48; social networking online, 40–43

Internal Revenue Service Web site, 80

Internet: finding information using, 16; using to move forward, 98–113

Internet downloads, 8

Internet filters, 56

Isolation, of online education, 106

J

Job hunting online, vii, 67–71; applications, 70; applications, 68; big search engines, 69; career history, 69; contact details, 68; education/qualifications/training, 69; going online, 68, 69, 71; headhunters/recruiters, 69; job search, 67–68; job-search sites, 69; job-specific search engines, 69; major achievements, 69; managing responses, 70; networking, 69; online classified ads, 69; post-hiring, 68, 70; preparation, 68; profile, 69; regional search engines, 69; resume, 67; tips for, 70–71; top employers, 69; vocabulary, 67

Job search, 67–68; sites, 69

L

Law enforcement, and your digital footprint, 36

Learner fit, and distance education, 106

Lesson format, xiii

Life skills online, 1–10, 59–80; additional resources, 2, 60, 82; communication online, 88–94; computer security, 3–10; income taxes, 77–80; job hunting, 67–71; lesson format, 1–2, 59–60, 81; money management with technology, 72–76; online forms, 83–87; public wireless access, 95–97; quiz, 60, 82; search skills, 61–66

Loans, 74; for online education, 113

M

Macro, 3

Malicious code, 3–4, 7–8

Metasearch engines, 63

MGM vs. Grokster, 56

Middle States Association of Colleges and Schools, 108

Money management online, 72–76; bill paying, 75; checkbook, balancing, 76; credit reports, 73; fraud, 76; loans, 74; vocabulary, 72

Myspace, 71

N

National Educational Technology Standards for Students (ISTE), viii–ix

Net pay/take-home pay, defined, 77

Netiquette, defined, 49

Networking, defined, 67

New England Association of Schools and Colleges, 108

Newbie, defined, 49

News Web sites, 17

Non-interrupting courses, in distance education, 106

North Central Association of Colleges and Schools, 108

Northwest Association of Schools and Colleges, 108

O

Offensive e-mail, 90

Ongoing security maintenance, banking online, 14

Online classified ads, 69

Online communication, *See* Communication online

Online education, vii, 105–109; accreditation, 107–108; applications, 111–113; benefits of, 105–106; cost of, 109; deadlines, 106; degree programs, 108; distance education, benefits of, 105–106; drawbacks of, 106; going online, 107–108; grants, 112–113; scholarships, 111–112; school loans, 113; stigma of, 106; student experience, 108–109; support services, 109; technical requirements, 109; work study, 113

Online forms, vii, 83–87; anonymity, 84; anti-virus/ anti-adware programs, selecting, 87; browser security options, setting, 85–86; cookies, 84–85; going online, 84; in pop-ups or on Web site home pages, 86; reaching others, 87; security of, 84; vocabulary, 83

Online persona, vi, 31–39; cause and effect, 37–38; digital footprint, 35–37; e-mail address, 32; free write, 31, 36; going online, 34; online personal safety and security maintenance, areas of, 31; personal information, 32; reaching others, 39; self-check, 38; user ID/screen name, 32; vocabulary, 31; Web site password protection, 34; Web site safety, tips for, 34

Opinion, defined, 16

Opt-in, defined, 83

Opt out, defined, 11

.org, 17

P

Packets, 5

Passive digital footprint, 35

Passwords: and banking online, 13; defined, 11, 31; security, 33; tricks, 33

Peer-to-peer (P2P) networking, vi, 54–58; anti-virus software/ firewall, 55; danger of, 56; defined, 54; file sharing, 54, 55; free write, 55; going online, 56; illegal uses of, 56; intellectual property, 55, 58; piracy, 56; pornographic downloads, 56; reaching others, 58; service overload, 55; spyware, 56; viruses, 56; vocabulary, 54

Pell Grant, 112

Perception, of online education, 106

Personal information: defined, 31, 83; and e-mail, 90; and online persona, 32; posting, 34

Personal Web site, 89

Pictures/photos, posting, 34

PINs, and banking online, 13

Pirated material, and peer-to-peer (P2P) networking, 56

Pornographic downloads, and peer-to-peer (P2P) networking, 56

Post-hiring, 70

Principles of Boolean logic, 64

Private information, 89

Public wireless access, vii, 95–97; activity, 96; firewall and, 95; free write, 97; hiding your files, 95; impact of going wireless, 96; privacy statement, 95; security precautions, 95; when to disable your wireless connection, 95

R

Reconciliation, defined, 72, 76

Regional accreditation, 107–108

Regional search engines, 69

Relationship, defined, 44

Relationships online, vi, 43–48, 44–48; dangers in forming, 44–45; formation of, 44; mnemonic, 45–46; safety tips on, 45; self-check, 48; types of online relationships, 46–47; vocabulary, 44

Reliable, defined, 16

Reputation, of online education, 106

Research, defined, 16

Research skills online, v, 16–20; evaluating a Web site, 18; inappropriate information, 17; inappropriate or extreme viewpoints, 17; potentially unsafe situations, 17; unreliable information, 17; URL, 17; vocabulary, 16; Web Site Evaluation Tool for Resources, 19–20

Retail shopping online, v, 21–28; benefits/negatives chart, 22; evaluating sites, 23–25; evaluation examples, 25–27; i-SAFE i-PARENT program, 28; protecting yourself, 22; Web Site Evaluation Tool for Online Shopping, 23

Right to freedom of speech, defined, 16

S

Safety tips, gaming online, 51

Scholarships, 111–112

School employees, and your digital footprint, 36

Schooling, viii: deadlines, 104; going online, 104; online applications, 104; options, 104; researching/selecting/ applying, 103–104

Screen name, 32; defined, 31

Script, 4

Search engine, defined, 77

Search skills online, vii, 61–66; activity, 63–64; activity extension, 64; advanced search forms, 64; combination search engines, 63; free write, 62; going online, 65; human-submitted search engines, 63; information searches, 62; multiple keywords, 64; phrase searching, 64; reaching others, 66; search engines, 62–63; search terms, 64; self-check, 65; simple + and/or — systems, 64; spidering, 62–63; topic overview, 77; topic/subject directories, 63; vocabulary, 77

Secure, defined, 11

Security prevention measures, 5–6

Security signs, and banking online, 13

Self-directed learners, and distance education, 106

SKU, defined, 83

Social interaction, and online education, 106
Social networking, 90–91; defined, 40, 88
Social networking online, vi, 40–43; alternate e-mail addresses, 42; anonymous post blocking, 42; comments, permanent recording of, 41; E-mail address hiding, 41; filtering options, 42; free write, 43; going online, 42; IP address logging, 42; password protection, 41; privacy features, 41–42; private communities, 42; reaching others, 43; risks posed by, 41; self-check, 43; social networking benefits, 42; vocabulary, 40
Social Security tax (FICA), 77
Software firewalls, 6
Southern Association of Colleges and Schools, 108
Spam, 90
Spidering, 62–63
Spyware, 4; and peer-to-peer (P2P) networking, 56
Spyware protection software, 5, 8–9
Stalking/harassment, 91
Streaming video, 34
Student experience, and online education, 108–109
Support services, and online education, 109
System updates, 4

T

Take-home pay, defined, 77
Tax preparation software, 79
Teacher's guide, xii
Technical requirements, online education, 109
Topic/subject directories, 63
Trojan horse, 3, 7–8
TRUSTe, defined, 77
Truth-in-Lending Act (Regulation Z), 14

U

URL, 17; defined, 11
User ID, 32; defined, 31

V

Valid, defined, 16
Virtual, defined, 11
Virus, 4
Viruses, and peer-to-peer (P2P) networking, 56

W

W-2 form, defined, 77
W-4 form, defined, 77
Web browser, defined, 77
Web, defined, 88
Web Site Evaluation Tool: for online shopping, 23; for resources, 19–20
Web site safety, tips for, 34
Webcam, 34
Western Association of Schools and Colleges, 108
What Do I Want to Be? (lesson), 100–102; brainstorming chart, 101; career correlations, 101; decision making, 102; free write, 102; going online, 101; knowing yourself, 100; offline research, 102; research, 101
Windows Firewall, 6
Windows operating system (OS) updates, 4, 5, 6–7
Wireless networks, vii, 92–94; activity, 94; denial of service (DOS) attack, 93; encryption, 94; home networks, 93–94; MAC address, 94; protecting, 93–94; reaching others, 94; routers, 94; setting up, 92
Wireless router, 6
Work study, and online education, 113
World Wide Web (WWW), defined, 88
Worm, 4, 7